I Feel A Little Jumpy Around You

I FEEL A LITTLE

JUMPY AROUND YOU

Paired Poems by Men & Women

Naomi Shihab Nye and *Paul B. Janeczko,* editors

ALADDIN PAPERBACKS

First Aladdin Paperbacks edition January 1999
Copyright © 1996 by Naomi Shihab Nye and Paul B. Janeczko
ALADDIN PAPERBACKS
An imprint of Simon & Schuster Children's Publishing Division
1230 Avenue of the Americas, New York, NY 10020
Pages 247–256 constitute an extension of this copyright
Also available in a Simon & Schuster Books for Young Readers hardcover edition.
Book design by Heather Wood / The text for this book is set in Horley Old Style
Printed and bound in the United States of America
1 3 5 7 9 10 8 6 4 2

The Library of Congress has cataloged the hardcover edition as follows:
Nye, Naomi Shihab.
I feel a little jumpy around you : a book of her poems and his poems presented in pairs
Edited by Naomi Shihab Nye & Paul B. Janeczko—1st ed.
p.   cm.   Includes index.
Summary : A collection of poems, by male and female authors, presented in pairings that
offer insight into how men and women look at the world, both separately and together.
ISBN 0-689-80518-7
1. Children's poetry, American—Women authors. 2. Children's poetry, American—men authors.
3. Women—Juvenile poetry. 4. Men—Juvenile poetry. [1. American poetry—Women authors—
Collections. 2. American poetry—Men authors—Collections. 3. Women—Poetry.
4. Men—Poetry.] I. Janeczko, Paul B. II. Title.
PS3564.Y44I4   1996   808.81—dc20   95-44904
ISBN 0-689-81341-4 (Aladdin pbk.)

The title of the collection *I Feel a Little Jumpy Around You* is taken from the poem "Jump City"
by Harryette Mullen on page 95. This poem first appeared in her collection *Tall Women* (1981).

A note on the cover paintings:
Deborah Maverick Kelley and Anthony Russo did not see each other's paintings until
the dust jacket for the hardcover edition of this book was printed, nor did they discuss
the subject matter for the art. Deborah's painting existed as a finished piece, and
Anthony was commissioned to paint a picture of a cake, a bride, and a groom.

A note on the running dialogue:
Naomi Shihab Nye and Paul B. Janeczko did most of their work on this volume by fax.
Excerpts from those faxes are printed on page 23, and on pages 219-246.

For Joan Darby Norris and Barry Norris,
my favorite she/he duet from way back when

–N.S.N.

With love, for Mary,
a sister whose formative years were enriched
by the four best brothers a girl could hope for.
There's no need to thank us

–P.B.J.

Contents

Heads on Fire

Foreign Exchange

The Real Names of Everything

Separate Longings

Introductions

Growing up in New Jersey in the 50's, my heroes included Willie Mays, Abbott and Costello, Sid Caesar, and Tommy Acker, a classmate of mine in seventh grade, who got a nun to faint with his patented Acker Attack, i.e., sliding out of his desk to the floor and rolling his eyes up into his head. My father—a 50's dad: aloof, hard working, stolid—wasn't my hero, although he should have been because of the lessons I learned from him. That happened years later when I came to understand what he did for my mother and his five kids. No women were my heroes. Not my mother. She was . . . my mom, and moms weren't heroes. Not in the 50's. Most of them, like mine, stayed at home and coped with being a housewife. Little did I know the heroic efforts it takes to do that job well.

My family came in two stages. The first included my parents and my two brothers and me, born within a five-year span. Long before Bruce Springsteen, my father was The Boss. He was the breadwinner, which frequently meant working a couple of jobs. Until early high school, my best friends were my brothers. We played ball together for endless hours. We watched out for each other. One of us would always stand lookout while the others scampered onto the school roof looking for lost baseballs. We served mass together. We delivered papers together. And we got in trouble together.

Another brother joined our merry band when we were seven, nine, and eleven. He was, of course, welcomed by us. I'm sure my mother, tiring of the antics of four boys, must have desperately craved for a sister of the soul. She got her wish two years later when our sister was born. Arriving a few days after Halloween, her birth did little to distract us from our trick-or-treat goodies.

Although my brothers and I enjoyed mistreating her when we were growing up, we were also fiercely protective of her. *We* could tease and hassle her, but if anyone else tried that, he (or she) would have to answer to us. And that went for her dates, who were often "interviewed" by my brothers or me before she could leave the house with them. Although my sister claims she never wanted or needed us to intervene in such a way, my brothers and I know that secretly she was touched by our concern.

Despite my traditional upbringing, I've been able to discard many of the macho shackles of the 50's. I do most of the cooking, even asking, on occasion, for my wife to leave "my" kitchen. I'm satisfied being *a* breadwinner. I believe that there are differences between men and women, but they shouldn't stop my daughter from pursuing whatever passions seize her soul.

Don't ask me how I was able to make that change. Like most important changes, this one has many causes. A major one is my wife, a strong woman—a hero for the work she does for abused children—who takes (and deserves) much credit for showing me the light. And my daughter, who, by spreading her energetic magic, demands that I pay attention to her as well as to my feminine side. And the times. They've changed a great deal since the days when I didn't bother to think much about the differences between men and women. The "men's movement" has made it more acceptable for a male to question his role in society.

The time is right for me to put together this collection of poems because it is about perceptions. How men and women poets perceive the world, their feelings, and themselves. And, how we perceive each other. Many of these poems surprised me because they were not what I expected to hear from a man or a woman. From that surprise came the delight of having my expectations shaken up, of being shown that there is room for me to grow and learn.

Reading poetry, by men and women, continues to make a difference in my life. It sensitizes me to the feelings of others. And it helps me to face many of my own feelings. I agree with Philip Booth, who said that a good poem "makes the world more habitable . . . [it] changes the world slightly in favor of being alive and being human." What other reason do we need for making poetry a vital part of our lives?

Paul B. Janeczko

When I was growing up in St. Louis, the geographical heart of the United States, I never felt any particular power exercised over me because I was female. No one ever said, "You can't do this because you're a girl," or "You shouldn't do that . . ." "The world felt inviting and open, and the possibilities of my life as richly various as any boy's on the block.

Despite the fact that my father came from what many people might identify as a patriarchal Middle Eastern culture (Palestinian), he seemed to have transcended the old roles of his heritage in my upbringing. I did feel my independent-minded, articulate mother "standing up for women's choices" (when I wanted to work on a farm picking berries with a bunch of boys, for example) more than once, which I will always appreciate. But other women of her generation probably also had to speak up this way, even with native-born American husbands.

I *was* aware that women "didn't have it so easy" in other parts of the world. Perhaps I was twelve before I seriously *contemplated* being a girl. And then it was only because of that gloomy "girl talk" they gave us in health class. . . .

My brother and I both liked reading, music, riding bicycles, baseball in the back lot. We both made pot holders on little red looms. He was a soprano; I was an alto. Although he played with matchbox cars while the treasure of my early years was a life-size doll, such distinctions seemed insignificant. We were a closely knit tribe, and equally mischievous. I might have said, as late as high school or college, that boys and girls were constitutionally the same.

Now, as a mother and wife, I would not say that. Even if boys and girls are the same for brief eras, it's obvious men and women aren't. I would arm-wrestle over this. I realize I walk a fragile crust of earth even identifying any differences *(look out!)*, and surely there are many exceptions:

Women often *do* like to talk more and to more people in quick succession, than men do, and their conversations often adhere to less literal patterns. They will talk about their relationships. It would be weird *not* to talk about their relationships. Feelings of all kinds are a legitimate realm for discussion—women's words travel there easily, and poke around, and don't mind what they touch.

Less is silly to women. Women honor the tiny, the tedious, the particular minutia. *(Exactly which B vitamin was it I read about?)* Women may have greater tolerance for *things*, which may have some connection to their frequent maintenance of *things*.

Men seem to respect the word *objective* more than many women do. Some seem to have a larger appetite for the abstract and the rational—let's face it, the dull.

Women seem to work quite well in a layered fashion (doing ten things at once), whereas men often feel more comfortable working in a linear mode—A to Z through a project. This has something to do with the ways we think, as well.

Women give each other neck massages at dinner parties without feeling embarrassed. They fling an easy arm around a shoulder. They are very flexible. It's not that hard to apologize when you have hurt someone's feelings.

Men do not get together to trade their clothes.

Men are more inclined to pitch their children into swimming pools—*(Come on, you can do it!)*—than women are.

Men have terrific broad perspectives. I get in trouble when I don't aim my Letters to the Editor past my husband before mailing them. He can always say, standing back calmly from my outrage, just where I should have added another line.

Women have immense strength of all kinds. Strength of attention, for instance—note a mother whose children interrupt her nineteen times during the telling of one tale, how she boomerangs back into the sentence she flew out of and continues. . . . Endurance, resilience, adherence, allegiance, patience—women have many middle names.

Women like details.

Women *are* details.

• • •

But then I contemplate—would we really want to be more alike, even if we could be? Do distinctions give us pleasure as well? I think of the realms in which we echo or play harmonious counterpoint, at least—our dreams, our disappointments, our attempts to make language convey our lives to ourselves and to one another. I cannot imagine we are that much different there.

Sometimes we construct bridges to link ourselves, or walls to stand us apart. Poet Robert Bly writes:

> Men wrong women, because a woman wants the two things
> Joined, but the man wants sawn boards,
> He wants roads diverging, and jackdaws flying,
> Heaven and earth parted. Women wrong men,
> Because the woman wants doves returning at dusk,
> Clothes folded, and giants sitting down at table.
> One wants the eternal river—which one? And the other wants
> A river that makes its own way to the ocean.

I think about this. Which one? Is it a changing one?

When Paul Janeczko and I started talking about this book, we liked the idea of pairing poems by male and female writers, putting two poems together that would suggest different or similar ways of approaching particular subjects and experiences. *Growing Up and Having Parents, Falling In and Out of Love, Contemplating the World, The Ongoing Human Longings We Carry Around with Us . . .* We liked the ideas of poems "having partners" within the book, so readers would be invited to read both poems together, considering their ties or tensions.

We called it the He/She book, or the She/He book, depending on who was talking. And we wondered, did anything interesting happen in the place between the poems? Did they link, or balance, or oppose, or set off little sizzles, by way of being together? Maybe they could shed extra light on one another sometimes. Maybe, in the energy and interaction between them, a third poem might be created.

And did gender have anything to do with it?

Sometimes we weren't sure. We argued. We changed our minds twice over the same poems. We interpreted perspectives variously. We had no idea how many great poems we would find that seemed perfect for this collection. And of course we didn't limit ourselves to our own genders in our searches.

We came to this project from different angles and corners of the country. Paul has a daughter, I have a son. He's a lifelong sports fan. I was a Spurs basketball fan for one season only, but it took too much out of me. Paul thinks poems in translation are like "driving used cars." I have never driven anything but used cars and I trust them. Paul and his family live in a new house in the woods in Maine. My family and I live in an old house in the inner city of San Antonio. Basically we called ourselves the "dueling anthologists."

As we worked on this book, snow piled up in his woods as the splendid seventy-five-degree blue-sky days of Texas winter surrounded me. I wouldn't let him forget it.

Paul sent me a tape called "Driving Home" (Philo Records), by one of his favorite singer/songwriters, Cheryl Wheeler. I quickly became addicted to her songs and played it over and over. "Bad Connection" made me laugh, thinking of our project and some of the issues it had raised. "She says they don't talk enough/He feels like she talks too much/She cites her years of patience/In all their conversations/He sits down, turns TV up/She's talking but he's not listening/He's heard it a thousand times/He tells her but she won't hear him/She listens between the lines . . ."

We hope you will listen between the lines and poems of this book but also TO the lines and images themselves, to feel how many intriguing contrasts and connections there can be between the multitudes of hes and shes.

Naomi Shihab Nye

"While there are men and women there will always be messes. Men are fire, women: patches of burlap. Things will happen."

—*Camilo Jose Cela*

Naomi: Paul, do you realize how many faxes you have sent me that say, "No more poems, please!" What is your problem? Not enough logs on the fire? Isn't it better to have too many to choose from rather than too few? How long does it take you to read a poem, anyway? It's a good thing this project is almost finished, otherwise we might not be speaking to each other anymore. Well, sorry I can't send you enchiladas by mail. Never mind the lobsters. I keep thinking about how they look in those tanks waving their hands.

Paul: It's hard to believe we are almost there. Of course, every office supply store for miles is out of fax paper. I swear the poems are flying out of my fax machine faster than paper towels in the rest room at Fenway Park during a Yankees game. I apologize if I bark at you for your endless questions. Actually, I prefer them to your constant taunting about your balmy weather while my mustache freezes on the walk down my driveway to the mailbox. By the way, kiddo, lobsters don't have hands. They're called claws, and they're rubberbanded shut to keep the lobsters—the female lobsters especially, from what I hear—from attacking each other in the tank.

Naomi: I don't particularly like being called "kiddo."

Reflections

Looking for myself,
I creep from one reflection to the next.
I stare; I see
suggestions of my son, my granddaughter.
I'm not there,

though if I should bend this way, and this
couldn't I curve back to the place
where the first mirror surely held me
in perfect, infinite, loving regard?

I'm drawn to any gleaming surface
—the polished floor, a silver horn,
windows in a revolving door.
They're never right, never
that milk-blue light I'm longing for.

Often I'm only smudges,
or scattered by cracks;
but I'm there at least,
I've some hold on the ground inhabited
before I found out what I lacked,
and what the mirror did.
And what the mirror
did.

Carole Satyamurti

Heads on Fire

 Galway Kinnell   Julie M. Convisser

Two Set Out on Their Journey

We sit side by side,
brother and sister, and read
the book of what will be, while the wind
blows the pages over—
desolate odd, desolate even,
and otherwise. When it falls open
to our own story, the happy beginning,
the ending happy or not we don't know,
the ten thousand acts which encumber
and engross all the days between,
we will read every page of it,
for if the ancestors have pressed
a love-flower for us, it will lie
between pages of the slow going,
where only those who adore the story
can find it. When the time comes
to close the book and set out,
whether possessing that flower
or just the dream of it, we will walk
hand in hand a little while,
taking the laughter of childhood
as far as we can into the days to come,
until we can hear, in the distance,
another laughter sounding back
from the earth where our next bodies
will have risen already

and where they will be laughing,
gently, at all that seemed deadly serious once,
offering to us new wayfarers
the light heart
we started with, but made of time and sorrow.

Galway Kinnell

Over the Pass

(for C.D.C. 1992)

The shattered tree tops crackle beneath our feet
like a nightmare, the delicate green fruit crushed
against the butt and backbone of the next fallen pine.
We climb over these, you leading,
straddling first, the branches, then the spongy, black trunks.
This is the path, you insist,
Look, to either side is thick forest, impossible in snow.
And I follow, watching my hands bleed
with bark-mud, slipping into nets of pine needles,
toes rattling like pebbles in my soaked boots.
No matter what else has happened, we know
you are the brother, and older.

At some point you are ready to turn back
and find the real path, the one that cuts like a stream
through the rearing hemlock up to Bald Mountain.
Now, because we are wet, we keep moving,
even though we have broken through the snow shield
and the sun is streaming over us.

We crest the pass and it comes: the white rush
of Mt. Hood in blue air. For whole minutes
we are still, side by side,

before we bicker about the return trail,
before skidding down the mountain,
cold stroking our skin like a long-fingered hand.
Before the tires of the pick-up spin out
so I inhale quick and you're impatient
with such ready lack of confidence,
before we re-enter my house, and you recount the hike
to my lover, leaving out what is important:
how in the beginning you persevered,
however strangely,
in that garden of fallen-down trees;
how I kept up.

Julie Convisser

 David Ignatow   Mary Jo Schimelpfenig

The Sky Is Blue

Put things in their place,
my mother shouts. I am looking
out the window, my plastic soldier
at my feet. The sky is blue

and empty. In it floats
the roof across the street.
What place, I ask her.

David Ignatow

A Geography of Lunch

My mother asks me if I like my sandwich.
I say I haven't tasted it yet.
"What are you doing? Are you dreaming
off into space?" she says.
I am doing nothing, mother.
I am writing.
I am writing it all down
and remembering the woman I will become.

I lift my sandwich, sinking teeth into toasted wheat.
I locate the precise taste of ham in my mind.
I eat slowly, like my grandmother, who savors her salad
as everyone inhales dessert.
I chew the poem forming,
mozzarella and words traveling the impossible road
to daylight.

Mary Jo Schimelpfenig

B. Vincent Hernandez   Paulette Jiles

Sunday

Sunday morning
while the Earth
arches below the sun

Mother washes dinner dishes
clanging silver spoons
as father pulls
nickels from our ears

There is really magic
in my head
and the ringing of silver
reminds me of
ice cream trucks
in the summer

Mother demands
that we stop these games
and calls our father
a fool.

                                        B. Vincent Hernandez

Paper Matches

My aunts washed dishes while the uncles
squirted each other on the lawn with
   garden hoses. Why are we in here,
I said, and they are out there?
   That's the way it is,
   said Aunt Hetty, the shriveled-up one.

I have the rages that small animals have,
being small, being animal.
   Written on me was a message,
"At Your Service,"
like a book of paper matches.
One by one we were taken out
and struck.
   We come bearing supper,
our heads on fire.

Paulette Jiles

 Agha Shahid Ali   *Robin Boody Galguera*

Snowmen

My ancestor, a man
of Himalayan snow,
came to Kashmir from Samarkand,
carrying a bag

of whale bones.
His skeleton
carved from glaciers, his breath
arctic,
he froze women in his embrace.
His wife thawed into stony water,
her old age a clear
evaporation.

This heirloom,
his skeleton under my skin, passed
from son to grandson,
generations of snowmen on my back.
They tap every year on my window,
their voices hushed to ice.

No, they won't let me out of winter,
and I've promised myself,
even if I'm the last snowman,
that I'll ride into spring
on their melting shoulders.

Agha Shahid Ali

Alloy

Once I tried to be Anglo, played up
my auburn hair, freckles, glad
my father was the Irishman
for the name. Felt ashamed by

my Tuscan nose, Mediterranean ancestors,
the words Ellis Island, second generation.

Now I embrace the Latin roots,
announce that fifty percent is Italian.
Being Catholic is good again.
But the freckles still reappear each
spring, the fair skin burning
in equatorial sun.

Some mornings when facing
the mirror, reflecting my Cherokee
great grandmother, the herbalist
who married a rancher from Texas
and gave birth thirteen times, the eyes
I claim as mine belong
to her, the flat fingernails a sure sign,
my father says.

What will my daughter
abandon to suit her lover's tastes?
I hope she embraces all, rejects
her mother's foolishness,
finds someone worthy of the souls
who breathe through her spectrum skin.

Which ghosts will claim me,
whose language can I speak?

Robin Boody Galguera

Philip Schultz *Chana Bloch*

For My Father

Samuel Schultz, 1903–1963

Spring we went into the heat of lilacs
& his black eyes got big as onions & his fat lower lip
hung like a bumper & he'd rub his chin's hard fur on my cheek
& tell stories: he first saw America from his father's arms
& his father said here he could have anything if he wanted it
with all his life & he boiled soap in his back yard & sold it door to door
& invented clothespins shaped like fingers & cigarette lighters
that played *Stars & Stripes* when the lid snapped open.

Mornings he lugged candy into factories
& his vending machines turned peanuts into pennies
my mother counted on the kitchen table & nights he came home
tripping on his laces & fell asleep over dinner & one night
he carried me outside & said only God knew what God had up His sleeve
& a man only knew what he wanted & he wanted a big white house
with a porch so high he could see all the way back to Russia
& the black moon turned on the axis of his eye & his breath
filled the red summer air with the whisky of first light.

The morning his heart stopped I borrowed money to bury him
& his eyes still look at me out of mirrors & I hear him kicking
the coalburner to life & can taste the peanut salt on his hands
& his advice on lifting heavy boxes helps with the books I lug town to town
& I still count thunder's distance in heartbeats as he taught me & one day
I watched the sun's great rose open over the ocean as I swayed on the bow

of the Staten Island Ferry & I was his father's age when he arrived
with one borrowed suit & such appetite for invention & the bridges
were mountains & the buildings gold & the sky lifted backward
like a dancer & her red hair fanning the horizon & my eyes burning
in a thousand windows & the whole Atlantic breaking at my feet.

Philip Schultz

Primer

1.

On the kitchen table, under
a dusting of flour, my mother's hands
pressed pastry into the fluted shell
with experienced thumbs.

Mustard-plaster, mercurochrome wand,
blue satin binding of the blanket
I stroked to sleep,
soft tar roof where the laundry
bellied and bleached,
sky veined with summer lightning:

If we were so happy,
why weren't we happy?

2.

Dreams sink a deep shaft down
to that first shoe,
bronzed, immortal.

We looked up at a sky of
monumental nostrils, grim tilted
backlit faces.

We learned to shape the letters,
l's and t's looped and tied, small i's
fastened by a dot.

When we stood up, our feet reached the ground,
We wiped the kisses from our cheeks with the backs of our
    hands.

    3.

I thought I was a grasshopper
in the eyes of giants.
My father set his hand on the doorknob,
slowly, without looking at me;
my mother lifted her hand, the fingertips
Hot Coral.
I thought she was saying Come here.

That's why I kept calling them back: *Look,
look who I've become!*
But it was too late;
he had his jacket on, and she
was smiling at her mouth in the hall mirror.

Now I am huge. This is my
bunch of keys, my silence, my own
steep face. These

are my children, cutting on the dotted lines:
blunt scissors
and a terrible patience.

Chana Bloch

 William Stafford   Linda Besant

Vocation

This dream the world is having about itself
includes a trace on the plains of the Oregon trail,
a groove in the grass my father showed us all
one day while meadowlarks were trying to tell
something better about to happen.

I dreamed the trace to the mountains, over the hills,
and there a girl who belonged wherever she was.
But then my mother called us back to the car:
she was afraid; she always blamed the place,
the time, anything my father planned.

Now both of my parents, the long line through the plain,
the meadowlarks, the sky, the world's whole dream
remain, and I hear him say while I stand between the two,
helpless, both of them part of me:
"Your job is to find what the world is trying to be."

William Stafford

Telepathy

Mom made me dust the living room while
she vacuumed the Chinese rug and
polished a silver plate for the cake.
Then we had a big fight but I lost so I
have to wear my new party outfit she's been
sewing for weeks with the crinkly
skirt and the black velvet vest and
bows in my braids plus
even my shiny shoes and
stupid socks with pink ribbons around the top.

All the party guests are playing
boring BINGO. Mamma hollers,
"Come inside," but I can't move.
A grasshopper is standing in my hand,
doing little pushups with her
perfect tiny legs.
"Teach me, teach me," I beg,
pinning my hopes on my own strong thighs.
"I want to jump off. I have to see
what's out there past the sky."

Linda Besant

Samuel Hazo   Linda Curtis Meyers

Yellow Delicious

From branching chandeliers they bell,
   drop and dribble still
   as tennis balls.
               The overripe
batter the ground in a smatter
of pulp.
             The rest, malshaped
as peppers cored by wasps
or worms but coming crookedly
to term, swing high
and green . . .
              I did my summer
best with watersoaks
and sprays.
           I planted stakes
of vitamins full circle
at the drip line.
             Nothing worked . . .
Shrugging, I watch the leaves
   curl brittle in September's fire.
I see the limbs and crown
   revert to architecture that will
   sleep the snowfalls and persist.
That's mystery enough for me.
Next summer means another tree.

Samuel Hazo

The Apple-Eater

(for my mother)

My sister and I used to tease her
about the apple cores.
Away at school,
we thought our rooms
should remain empty—
the sunlight alone on the bed,
dust particles hovering
in warm air. Somewhere
in the recesses of her day—
the cleaning done, dinner
a distant thought—she'd open
one of our doors, an apple
in one hand, a book
in the other. I don't know how
she chose the room. Perhaps
she followed the sun's movement
across the house, as it visited
each room with an hour of intensity.
I see her against a pillow, hear
the snap of apple skin, the soft flutter
of pages. While we were gone
she read all of Fitzgerald and Hemingway,
most of Faulkner. I'd come home
to a slightly rumpled bed,
one browning core
on the headboard. Even then,
I knew she was not
inconsiderate. She'd left

in a rush to make dinner, the characters
still talking, the apple
eaten down to seeds,
stem, the slenderest
of cores.

Linda Curtis Meyers

 Robert Farnsworth   Edith Södergran

Coloring Book

The strawberries lie in a dish of cream.
The man has chosen them, pulled
their green crowns off and halved
their whole red hearts with a knife.

Feast your eyes, he says. He knows
to seek the world at its ripest.
But the child, confronted with page after page
of empty outlines, is puzzled.

If she learns that in April strawberries
are tiny green replicas of strawberries,
does she ignore what her bitter tongue
has told her, and color them green?

She turns the page. The blue egg at the foot
of the oak outside is her secret. It is empty.

She wonders what left it, and if it lived.
From where she sits by the window,

the yard with the oak and her bicycle seems
smaller than it is. In the coloring book
there is nothing like her life but one hatched
egg. She colors it blue. The man says that once

he rowed home under clouds with a flounder
that swam in a bucket of gravel and water.
While he watched, it colored itself like stones
and bits of shale. He wished he'd had a bucket

of quartz so he'd have gotten a fish
like a rusting moon. But dead it turned an evil
umber anyway. They share the strawberries. He
tells her about a Frenchman who lived on a flatboat

every summer, painting the river Seine, the sky
within the river, the water flowers and the quays.
This, the man says, was an act of love. Thinking
of love, and the crayons spread across the table,

he is happy with the world. Things he tells her,
have an order we don't yet understand. Even
the traffic lights turn green to yellow to red all
night, though no one is there to obey them.

Robert Farnsworth

On Foot I Had to Walk Through the Solar Systems

On foot
I had to walk through the solar systems,
before I found the first thread of my red dress.
Already, I sense myself.
Somewhere in space hangs my heart,
sparks fly from it, shaking the air,
to other reckless hearts.

Edith Södergran
Translated by Stina Katchadourian

 Walter McDonald   Denise Duhamel

The Pee Wee Coach

I ring the doorbell and wait, cap on my head
and grinning. They open the storm door wide,
believing my T-shirt, my pocket tucks,
the lineups and plays on my clipboard.

They hope I'll prove I'm good, so I shake hands
with both, as if baseball's an exclusive
summer camp and I'm here to see if her little one
is worthy. The kid comes out, skinny and short,

or fat, nothing at six hinting baseball but his Keds.
If he whines, clings to his mother or won't talk,

I put him in right field where he'll be safe
to dream and pinch himself and pee. I say

I'm proud to have him, and practice is at four.
I field their questions, legs wide apart,
clipboard crossed on my chest as if I know
secrets of how their son can bat .400.

I give the talk about how baseball's not
just playing hard and winning, but having fun
and learning to be men. But I drop hints
of titles the teams I've coached have won,

the names of boys I've helped win scholarships
to college. I say I feel we've got the boys
to win the pennant. By then they're ready
for sweat and tears, or sitting on the bench

if that will do it—all but the boy,
who sees me as I am, a man with a stopwatch
on his wrist, hairy, selling something
to his folks, a coach who probably has boys

already picked to play, guys who can hit
and spit and tell jokes about his sisters
and his mother, the things it takes
to be a big boy in the world.

Walter McDonald

Feminism

All over the world, Little Bees, Star Scouts,
and Blue Birds play Telephone, whispering messages
in a chain link of ears—no repeating (that's cheating),
only relaying what they hear their first shot.
Sometimes "Molly loves Billy" becomes "A Holiday in Fiji,"
or "Do the Right Thing" becomes "The Man Who Would Be King."
Still, there is trust. Girls taking the Blind Walk,
a bandanna around one's eyes (Pin the Tail on the Donkey-style)
as another leads her through the woods
or a back yard or entire city blocks. Girls helping
where they are needed or inventing ways to aid
where they seemingly are not. Memorizing remedies
for cuts and stings, frostbite, nosebleeds.
Their motto: Be prepared at all times.
Full of anxiety, they watch for home hazards,
check for frayed toaster or hair dryer cords.
Outside they watch for color changes in cloud formations,
the darkening of the sky. They're safest in cars
during electrical storms.
                              There's so much to remember and learn.
So many impending disasters, yet so many well wishes
for their world. These girls shut the tap
as they brush their teeth, secure glow-in-the-dark reflectors
on their bikes, and do at least one good turn daily.
They are taught that alone they are small,
but if they can empathize with each other, they can gain power.
Just to see what it feels like, a walking girl
may spend an afternoon in a wheelchair. Another
may stuff cotton in her ears. And to be readied

for what lies ahead when they grow up
and they're no longer Girl Scouts, they make collages
cutting images from magazines showing what they might be:
mothers or lawyers, reporters or nurses.
Or they play Rabbit Without a House, a Brazilian form
of London Bridge, or American Musical Chairs.
There will always be an odd number of girls, always
one left out. The earth and her scarce resources.
Survival in Sudan begins with Sheep and Hyena.
And though all the girls may try to protect the one
who is the Sheep in the middle of their circle, most often
the outside Hyena does not give up
and breaks through sore forearms and weakened wrists
to eat her. Red Rover, Red Rover,
it is better when Girl Scouts stay together.
So they bond tightly in their Human Knot,
a female version of a football team's huddle.
And all holding hands, they squeeze their Friendship Squeeze,
knowing each small one-at-a-time grip
is like a Christmas tree light, each a twinkle
the rest of the strand cannot do without.
Each missing face on the missing child poster
like the fairest of all looking into her mirror.

Denise Duhamel

Moshe Dor *Robin Boody Galguera*

Before Sleep

1.

Before sleep Baba arranges extra
blankets on her feet. "The weight,"
she explains, "will keep me
from flying." Walnut trees
hold still in the garden.

2.

Baba sleeps, her cheek pressed
to the pillow, her hair flowing.
In the garden walnut trees
turn silvery.

3.

In silence I shall steal
to her bedside, dismantle
the burdens of her life, then turn
my back and tiptoe away. Baba
is flying, above walnut trees, above
wandering souls. She soars
higher than milky ways and choirs
of seraphim. When she returns,
her hair will be heavy
with the dust of stars.

Moshe Dor
Translated by Barbara Goldberg

Second Childhood

for Josephine Genovali

My grandmother, a few days from ninety
and deafened by the noise of her life,
turned to my mother and said, *Maybe I can get my old job*
back when we move to San Francisco.
Some piece of our dinner conversation
wound through the nautilus of her mind, rushed
her back to teenage years. The bay crossing
by ferry to work in a banner factory.
We ignored the way her memories,
like specks of dust under stark light,
float around a room.

I pulled a sepia portrait
from the leather album to frame
for her birthday. Corner holders fell
like black confetti. The face is the same: obsidian eyes,
angular jaw. I set the present on her dresser,
a few days later found the silver rectangle buried
under old flannel nightgowns, and left it there.

As she passes through days colored silently
pale, she feels those afternoons in Torre di Lago
when she lived next door to Puccini, his piano
billowing into Tuscan air.
The way her starched white dress
ballooned around her when an older sister
pushed her over a wall into cold water.

Robin Boody Galguera

Alberto Ríos   *Melody Lacina*

What a Boy Can Do

February, and the wind has begun
Milk cartons moving along the curb,
An occasional wrapper, Babe Ruth.

The young tree bends in a hoeing.
Cirrus clouds, sparrows, jet trailings:
Each puts a line on the sky. February

Kites, too, their shapes: the way three
Boys have taken their baseball fields
Into the air, flying them on strings.

When I flew my kite I shouted, louder,
Anything, strong, boy wild and rocks:
February was here. I was helping.

Alberto Ríos

Red Cross Lessons at City Park Pool

My mother never learned to swim, so we did,
my sisters and me, every summer
for two weeks. It was always early morning,
always cloudy. At the gate
someone dressed in something warm droned
name after name, getting most of them wrong.

They made us take showers
without heat. They made us wait
huddled on the deck, blue-lipped,
until our teachers said
get in. My oldest sister was
a natural, even took lifesaving and
synchronized swiming. She learned to sink
to music, one leg up like a periscope.
My other sister had a steady stroke.
I was afraid of the deep end
the summer I got Connie. Connie stood
dry on the lip of the pool, mean towel
cinched at her waist. Dark glasses shrouded
her eyes that could have been looking anywhere.
They were looking for mistakes.
I dreamed of the ten-foot marker, the diving boards
like knives. I said I was sick.
My mother said nothing. But next day
she tugged me from bed, determined.
Connie was still by the deep end.
To here, she said. The pool was a mouth
that could swallow me. I pressed
myself down the ladder, pried my fingers
from the rungs. Would my arms forget
everything? Connie watched me swim
past what I couldn't do. *To here.*

Melody Lacina

 *Alberto Ríos*   *E. K. Miller*

La Sequia

Peaches are drying up all around
Elfrida, Arizona. I must be
like my grandfather, without a sound
to show he's worried at all; his brown
hand rubs the elbow that feels like the
peaches are drying up all around
the pores and ridges of his skin and down
his back. My father used to do that; he,
like my grandfather, without a sound
of complaint, wore a fire that was blond
on his head. He too would say, *I can see*
peaches are drying up all around
through the blue-eyes bruises he gave me
like my grandfather, without a sound
gave him one summer, one night on the ground
ripping apart the only thing he could. The
peaches are drying up all around
like my grandfather, without a sound.

Alberto Ríos

My Father's Garden

He paced the length of it all day,
two rows of sweet corn, two of beans,

five rows of tomatoes, yellowed in the sun.
The scarce wind ruffled sheets out on the line,

its dry fingers soft as his grandmother's,
her light breath before she died. By August,

weeds choked out the plants and he would stay in bed,
his belly swollen, the broken corpuscles in his face

red with heat. At night, when it was cool
we climbed up to the hay mow and jumped down

to a mattress on the floor, first Bob, then Robin,
and I always last, always afraid.

My father could do anything to me, knock me down,
wake me in the middle of the night to cook a meal,

but nothing frightened me, nothing like how far away
that mattress was. Bob is gone. There is no garden.

But I am still up on the hay mow. My brother looks at me
expectantly. I stiffen, close my eyes. I always jump.

E. K. Miller

 David Huddle   Ruth Stone

Two Facts

My mother married when she was fifteen.
Her first child, a girl, died after two days.
My father, discussing religion with me,
said he'd "had a hard time" in his twenties.
I think about them. Stopped in reverie
I've held in mind this tableaux, this scene:
Faith lost, he sits beside her on the bed.
No child now, she can think only of the dead
child who would have been my older sister.
Though I never saw them so young, I know
how their faces look there, the light falling
in slats into that upstairs bedroom. I know
some of it. But I am afraid of feeling
how much they ache to say *daughter, daughter.*

David Huddle

Pokeberries

I started out in the Virginia mountains
with my grandma's pansy bed
and my Aunt Maud's dandelion wine.
We lived on greens and back-fat and biscuits.
My Aunt Maud scrubbed right through the linoleum.
My daddy was a northerner who played drums
and chewed tobacco and gambled.

He married my mama on the rebound.
Who would want an ignorant hill girl with red hair?
They took a Pullman up to Indianapolis
and someone stole my daddy's wallet.
My whole life has been stained with pokeberries.
No man seemed right for me. I was awkward
until I found a good wood-burning stove.
There is no use asking what it means.
With my first piece of ready cash I bought my own
place in Vermont; kerosene lamps, dirt road.
I'm sticking here like a porcupine up a tree.
Like the one our neighbor shot. Its bones and skin
hung there for three years in the orchard.
No amount of knowledge can shake my grandma out of me;
or my Aunt Maud; or my mama, who didn't just bite an apple
with her big white teeth. She split it in two.

Ruth Stone

 Robert Bly   *Andra Davis*

Taking the Hands

Taking the hands of someone you love,
You see they are delicate cages . . .
Tiny birds are singing
In the secluded prairies
And in the deep valleys of the hand.

Robert Bly

From Him

I got navy blue eyes that apologize
when looked into.

I got the shape of his hands, the fingers
that like to turn pages.

From his chest I got a space
full of white boney bars—a playground
and the ache
trying to make sense of

Andra Davis

 Eric Chock   *Kathryn Kerr*

The Belt

As I dressed for dinner tonight
I realized I was putting Daddy's
genuine snakeskin belt around my waist,
the one he used to feel was light enough
to wrap once around his fist
and with the free end hanging
whip my small child's body
around my bare legs
as I would run past him after sundown
late from finishing a football game

or wandering too long down an unexplored
tributary in the stream,
not even caring whether I missed dinner
which was nothing
on his plantation worker's salary.
I wonder if he felt
like the man on the horse then,
or if it even entered his mind
what he was passing on to me.

Eric Chock

Touch

Mother was a washcloth
smearing my face clean,
shoes tied to last all day,
the back of the hairbrush
on top of my head
if I wiggled
when it pulled.

Father was a knuckle
on my head at dinner time,
a snowball on the side of my face,
the force that lifted
me by one arm
while the yardstick
set me straight.

Kathryn Kerr

 Chuck Martin   Cill Janeway

Size Is Relative

Four years at school left me taller,
lots of luggage to take home, squeezed into
my father's car. But every mile from the airport
shrinks me smaller. Soon I'll fit my old room.

Chuck Martin

Rose

My cousin named her baby Rose.
Rose like a flower, like a deep red flower
everyone wants to smell, to touch, to tame.
When I think of Rose, I think of Rising
She Rises
    She Rose
        like the sun, like flying, like magic
like an angry woman rising out of the home.

Rose has a birthmark under her right eye;
it shines when she smiles.
When people stop to look at the child, they say
"Oh what a sweet baby,
    oh, but you could have that removed, you know
        it's very easy, you know."

And they will. They will try
as they have tried to pick every woman's Rose
they will try to take hers
try to keep her
    from knowing her name
        from   Rising.

Cill Janeway

 George Eklund   Liz Rosenberg

Boyhood Winter

We walked all that way to the water
in a boyhood winter
down to the huge frozen bay
where the long white hulls
had been pulled to safety.
Along the empty canal
the light was choked with cold
and we played hockey
nearly furious, nearly graceful
beneath the windows of the wealthy.

I had met a girl at school
and my mind was full and sleepy
and the name of her street was lovely and near.
I watched my younger brothers
laughing as they flailed
and slid away on their bellies

I gazed at the great houses
up and down the canal
just as the winter glare began
to twist itself around stucco corners
and then the rooms were lit
and the wealthy moved about
behind the orange glass
like ghosts upon a yacht
and in half my sleepy mind I believed
they were easy going and generous
and happy to lose their daughters.

George Eklund

A Suburban Childhood

Having a crush was how I existed—
how I spent recess; I wandered
dull fields gone brilliant
for one sullen boy who strolled scornfully by.
As if in a dream I boarded
strange buses, stepped down
and roamed through the flower-named
streets, past the one house lit up
from within; humming he loves me,
he loves me not yet . . .
past mounds of leaves burning
their acid of longing
till in the violet dusk headlights
would splash me; behind them my mother

propped up at the wheel—her mouth open,
the doors of the car flying out—
as she grabbed for me, already screaming.

Liz Rosenberg

 Mark Vinz   Maria Mazziotti Gillan

Sins of the Fathers

My daughter wants the car tonight, no,
needs the car tonight—to go somewhere,
to do some things, you know, be back
before it gets too late, of course,
if I say so, which I always do,
of course. I trust her—it's the others
I don't trust, the others I worry about,
and round we go again.

Headlights pass the driveway—
I study every shadow on the wall,
each voice from the dark street,
and laughter—faint, familiar
laughter, rising and falling
on every breath of wind.

Mark Vinz

My Daughter at 14: Christmas Dance, 1981

Panic in your face, you write questions
to ask him. When he arrives,
you are serene, your fear
unbetrayed. How unlike me you are.

After the dance,
I see your happiness; he holds
your hand. Though you barely speak,
your body pulses messages I can read

all too well. He kisses you goodnight,
his body moving toward yours, and yours
responding. I am frightened, guard my
tongue for fear my mother will pop out

of my mouth. "He is not shy." You giggle,
a little girl again, but you tell me he
kissed you on the dance floor. "Once?"
I ask. "No, a lot."

We ride through rain-shining 1 A.M.
streets. I bite back words which long
to be said, knowing I must not shatter your
moment, fragile as a spun-glass bird,

you, the moment, poised on the edge of
flight, and I, on the ground, afraid.

Maria Mazziotti Gillan

 *David Wevill*   *Judy Ruiz*

The Mystery

They said of my father: George was a good man.
They said of my mother: Sylvia was a saint.
But the people who said that sort of thing
are now almost gone. I recall
the bread they baked, the white aprons
the pipesmoke caught in wool, and those
long winters the bones never forget
that turn to names and dates engraved in stone.
Sometimes I thank God I never
knew my parents, yet loved them, and was loved.
Among the normal torments of being a child
I didn't need the griefs they hid from me.
What I am now lies in shadow. Could I, should I
speak of two dead lovers as my wound?

David Wevill

Gifts

I'd talk to them now,
bring warm drinks,
light the fire,
put on Vaughn Monroe's
"Racing with the Moon."

I'd say
this is where I live,
these are the trees
I see every morning,
this is the chair
where I sit while the sun
goes down,

this is the floor by my bed
where I kneel at night,
these are my slippers,
and this is the book I love the most.

I'd sing for my mother—
she always liked that;
and for my father
I'd never get old or fat.

I'd say, "Here, Daddy.
You put the angel on top of the tree."

Judy Ruiz

 Peter Desy   *Molly Peacock*

Father Falling

You stood there slack, with glassy
eyes reflecting the room, so drunk
you swayed, and I readied to catch you.

You wore a foolish grin, and a single bead
of drool hung from your chin. I wanted
to scold you, but I thought of the man
you were, and then I wanted to put you back
together piece by piece, like a broken
china vase—wrists, knees, elbows, vertebrae . . .
I thought "This is my father," and I could
barely move my brain beyond those words.
If you had fallen, you would have fallen
through my arms, heavier even than the light falling
that day through the window onto my bent shoulders.

Peter Desy

Our Room

I tell the children in school sometimes
why I hate alcoholics: my father was one.
"Alcohol" and "disease" I use, and shun
the word "drunk" or even "drinking," since one time
the kids burst out laughing when I told them.
I felt as though they were laughing at me.
I waited for them, wounded, remembering how I imagined they'd howl at me
when I was in grade 5. Acting drunk
is a guaranteed screamer, especially
for boys. I'm quiet when I sort the junk
of my childhood for them, quiet so we
will all be quiet, and they can ask what

questions they have to and tell about what
happened to them, too. The classroom becomes
oddly lonely when we talk about our homes.

Molly Peacock

 Phillip Lopate   *Penny Harter*

Once a Long Time Ago

Once a long time ago, you remember
we were living in the basement of our parent's house
we two brothers, the girls sharing a room upstairs
It was dark in the basement, dark and hard to move around
and our sister charged her friends a dime
to visit, calling it the Spook House.
    I would look up from my book
sometimes and see a line of ten year olds
in pink shorts
climbing down the trap door steps.
What are you doing here? I asked calmly
never realizing I was the spookiest part of all
The little girls giggled and ran for help
Maybe you don't remember that
You were too busy looking for a job

    Maybe you remember how we slept together
next to the oil burner
on an old double mattress, getting along,

two friends, never complaining about privacy
until one afternoon around four-thirty
I came across you, my older brother, older
and ashamed to be living under his mother's roof,
your legs hanging out of a green, sour-smelling topsheet,
your black hair mussed, your stallion's eyes desperate
like horses trapped in a flaming barn.
You wouldn't look at me.
                               I asked you what was wrong
you remember? But instead of answering your whole body shrunk
and when I got into bed beside you
you started to cry   you started to cry but no sound came out
and I was wondering if you were faking
or if there was so much that wanted to come out
that you had to hold a pillow over it
    and smother it
I never told you this but Esquire Magazine was lying
on the floor face up, the new issue, and I wondered
if something you had seen there had made you unhappy
like the disgusting Bourbon ads, or the dense novelettes
that left me slightly nauseous like cups of warm water

I also wished I could look at the new issue
I had time for many thoughts because you took a while crying
and I couldn't think of anything to do except hold you
and keep asking what was wrong
I felt confident in the end you would tell me
and this is perhaps what you could never forgive me
My conqueror's belief in the absolute power of sympathy
because you never did tell me
and I saw that you didn't trust me enough

and I still don't know to this day
what was wrong
because all you said was
"Leave me alone, just leave me alone for two minutes."

Phillip Lopate

Mattress Fire

When I was a child, my father
lit a cigarette in the night
and fell back asleep,
his arm dangling over the edge,
his curled fingers holding fire.

My parents dragged his mattress to the bathtub.
Later, they pinned an old blanket, tight
around its sagging middle
where some stuffing had dissolved to soggy
            lumps.

For years I watched my mother
change the sheets on that burnt mattress,
smoothing them over the old blanket,
the charred hole in the striped ticking.

My mother changed the sheets on that mattress
even when cancer from three packs a day
began to burn my father's jawbone,
dissolve his soft palate;

even after surgery, when he nestled
into his new life, his body
finding the familiar hollows.

The mattress finally collapsed into itself
twenty years after he stopped smoking.

Somewhere, my father's mattress still burns,
smouldering in the dumps off the Turnpike
like those underground fires
they can't put out for years.

Penny Harter

 James Laughlin   *Toi Derricotte*

Step on His Head

Let's step on daddy's head shout
the children my dear children as
we walk in the country on a sunny

summer day my shadow bobs dark on
the road as we walk and they jump
on its head and my love of them

fills me all full of soft feelings
now I duck with my head so they'll
miss when they jump they screech

with delight and I moan oh you're
hurting you're hurting me stop and
they jump all the harder and love

fills the whole road but I see it run
on through the years and I know
how some day they must jump when

it won't be this shadow but really
my head (as I stepped on my own
father's head) it will hurt really

hurt and I wonder if then I will
have love enough will I have love
enough when it's not just a game?

James Laughlin

The Struggle

We didn't want to be white—or did we?
What did we want?
In two bedrooms, side by side,
four adults, two children.
My aunt and uncle left before light.
My father went to the factory, then the cleaners.
My mother vacuumed, ironed, cooked,
pasted war coupons. In the afternoon
she typed stencils at the metal kitchen table.

I crawled under pulling on her skirt.
What did we want?
As the furniture became modern, the carpet deep, the white
ballerina on the mantel lifted her arms like some girl near
terror;
the Degas ballerinas bowed softly in a group, a gray sensual
beauty.
What did we push ourselves out of ourselves
to do? Our hands
on the doors, cooking utensils, keys; our hands
folding the paper money, tearing the bills.

Toi Derricotte

 Mark Vinz   Patty Turner

Passages

The first poem in the book
I just happen to open
is about a dead father—
how many like it I've read
before I knew what they meant.
And now, every book I pick up
has one of those poems in it—
every book in every room.

Listen: sometimes he and I would
sit alone, for hours, not talking.
I couldn't leave—he wanted me home,

not to talk to or listen to,
just to sit there, two aging men . . .
Do you know how it is
to hate somebody for leaving
when you need him there?

Mark Vinz

Looking for Him

Once in a while when I lean my head back to stare at the sky,
I am looking for him.
Today I'm looking, today when it's all gray.
The softest gray I've ever seen, this sky
opening after a rain and getting ready to close again
for another.
A light behind this sky
shimmies, gold above gray.
I try to see his soul up there floating around like
a thin blanket of human just under the clouds.
Or glimpse the wing of an angel,
a boy-angel playing in the gold-gray light
up above the clouds.
I try hard to see.
And then gray turns solid, light disintegrates.
I try to keep it inside my body, the light.
When I can,
he lays his hand on my shoulder.
Then I put my hand on his and say to no one,
"Daddy, oh Daddy."

Patty Turner

 William Stafford   Marlys West

Remembering Brother Bob

Tell me, you years I had for my life,
tell me a day, that day it snowed
and I played hockey in the cold.
Bob was seven, then, and I was twelve,
and strong. The sun went down. I turned
and Bob was crying on the shore.

Do I remember kindness? Did I
shield my brother, comfort him?
Tell me, you years I had for my life.

Yes, I carried him. I took
him home. But I complained. I see
the darkness; it comes near: and Bob,
who is gone now, and the other kids.
I am the zero in the scene:
"You said you would be brave," I chided
him. "I'll not take you again."
Years, I look at the white across
the page, and think: I never did.

William Stafford

The Exciting New Concept of Art Therapy

Dr. Stupid says
girls
we're going to try
something new today
here is some paper
and markers
draw a picture
of your house
and everybody in it.

However you like
to draw is fine
you can make it
any size
just be sure
and include everyone
in the family
I'll let you two alone
so you can
get creative.

Dr. Stupid leaves us
in the hospital playroom.

I say to my sister
let's draw everything
with thick black lines
and when you get
to your bedroom

make brown scribbles
everywhere

She says let's
put some blood
on the stairs
maybe big
knives in the kitchen
jumping out
of the drawers

We laugh and draw
our houses
bright and sunny

everybody's bedroom
with flower pots
the whole family
smiling
watering the plants

the sun is a big
smiley face too

Dr. Stupid looks at
our pictures
and says
we did a fine
job
he said
we're fine

and well adjusted
little girls
he kept the
pictures for
an article
or something

Dear Dr. Stupid
didn't you see
the dog outside
it was chained up
with a little
bone in his mouth

I tell my sister
that isn't me watering
flowers in the
bedroom
that's me
outside
in the dog's jaw.

My sister says
that's funny
I was the toilet
in the basement.

Marlys West

Li-Young Lee   *Lucia Casalinuovo*

A Story

Sad is the man who is asked for a story
and can't come up with one.

His five-year-old son waits in his lap.
Not the same story, Baba. A new one.
The man rubs his chin, scratches his ear.

In a room full of books in a world
of stories, he can recall
not one, and soon, he thinks, the boy
will give up on his father.

Already the man lives far ahead, he sees
the day this boy will go. *Don't go!*
Hear the alligator story! The angel story once more!
You love the spider story. You laugh at the spider.
Let me tell it!

But the boy is packing his shirts,
he is looking for his keys. *Are you a god,*
the man screams, *that I sit mute before you?*
Am I a god that I should never disappoint?

But the boy is here. *Please, Baba, a story?*
It is an emotional rather than logical equation,

an earthly rather than heavenly one,
which posits that a boy's supplications
and a father's love add up to silence.

Li-Young Lee

The Lizard's Tango

She was sleeping in the woodpile
when you caught her.
Now she plays dead on your palm,
blue belly up,
while you stand
on the white linoleum of the kitchen,

a small mountain lake
cupped in your hands,
your stiffened fingers
unwilling to drop any
of the precious water.
You have grown out of me

in silence,
as a persimmon tree grows in one's yard
and bears fruits without notice.
Your groin molds your jeans
the way your hands
mold the lizard against you;
your heart

a baby lizard dancing a tango,
a pebble
smoothing its way to the ocean.

I envy the lizard in your hands.

Lucia Casalinuovo

 Wing Tek Lum   *Karen Mitchell*

The Backup

"With nothing done to show for all those years"

—T'ao Ch'ien

She kneels behind her best friend
who also kneeling
has put on my extra large T-shirt
but with her arms
snuck down the inside of the shirt
and through an old pair of shorts
her hands stuffed
into my daughter's socks and shoes.
My daughter has run her arms
from under the back of the shirt
out through the arm holes.
With a beach towel
to hide her friend's lap
and a little stool
set underneath the shorts

they make it seem
as if a goofy midget has arrived
in our living room
with the face and voice of her friend.
She sings "Row Row Row Your Boat"
with raucous glee
and tells cornball jokes about a cow.
The friend kicks up the "legs"
as she wails away
and later crosses them repeatedly
while "sitting" on the stool.
My daughter waves the "arms"
and every so often pulls up the shorts
or sets back the stool
when it has overturned.
We laugh our heads off.
My daughter grins
and looks around with merry eyes.
I am filled with pride
and yet a touch of disappointment too
to see her once again
the backup for the star
as if this was all she wished to be.
I hold my tongue
as fellow parents have told me to.
It is just that I would hope for her
for something more
more than what her second-string father
could ever show
                    for all these years.

                                        Wing Tek Lum

Black Patent Leather Shoes

Slipping into my black patent leather shoes
Not caring how many others had worn them
Or how many times they'd been
Used
Papa would make me put them on
With lace stockings
I never danced in those black leather
Shoes
Only studied their simple details:
Black
As black as my hair they surely were
With three straps, that held me there, and heels
Stacked
And I could not wear my black leather
Shoes
Every day, but only once or twice a
Week
and he would make sure black polish was
Used
Papa would make sure those shoes
Reflected me

Karen Mitchell

Christopher Cokinos   M. Eliza Hamilton

Short-Wave

Nights, when I was a boy, my dad and I
would walk into the cold garage
lit by that single improbable bulb.
We would listen to the short-wave radio.
I couldn't imagine the gulf of air
between me and those voices
clipped with static, Radio Moscow's
English Service and the BBC,
and sounds I thought were French
or maybe Greek. I think those nights
he was building something
or taking something apart.
I remember how he promised
the powered airplane, a model
you could fly on a tether
in an orbit around yourself, flight
you could hold with your fingers, your hand.
He never finished, though one night
I found the station that only kept time:
a beep each second, a long beep each minute,
then the deep British voice intoning
the exact hour, minute and second
in Greenwich Mean Time, and I asked
why their time was different
from ours. Dad liked to explain
science—facts and rules,

principles that were always true,
hard as a vise, wood-solid, useless,
sheltering too, like the sad garage
of his failing marriage, where I also sat,
a child liking voices plucked from the dark.
They sounded patient and soothing, adult,
like a father carefully telling
how time works, in zones,
half the world already living
in tomorrow, telling this
to his son who couldn't understand, not then.

Christopher Cokinos

For My Father's Mother Who Has Alzheimer's

for Richard Timothy Hamilton

I.

Rightful retribution
I want to tell my father.
She who refused me entry into her past
now has no entry herself.
He says, somberly, It happened to my father too.
In the silence between us, his own fear is audible.
This is not about motherhood;
not about a woman he doesn't like because
she never acted Grandmother;
never did a lot of things he needed.
This is about History.

II.

From the West Coast of Africa
Slavers chain their captives carefully for maximum storage
and assured isolation.
No tribe together: No communication: No mutiny.
Sometimes.
Because language exists without words.
The body remembers its freedom.
The heart remembers home and will make you walk water to find it.

III.

This robbing of my life all over again.
Who will bear witness with no one left to speak the old ways?
What if I find a bill of sale for one ancestor?
What could it tell me?

> One young negress of 16 years
> purchased for $300.00
> will bear children
> healthy, strong field hand
> goes by the name of Susan.

This new world birth certificate is not
the beginning of her life.
What of the gold she wore around her ankles:
Was it sold in exchange for shackles?
What of the chants her Mothers taught her:
Did she forget them to save her tongue?
What of the trip back home:
Did she choose not to walk back with the others?

What of her name:
Did she know I would be born to remember her?

IV.

Things I know:
I am Cherokee;
I am Blackfoot;
I am Fulani.
The language of my people exists
between Guinea, the Middle Passage, and the reservations.
The history of my people is in its language.
The memory of my people has not been found.
My life will create it.

V.

My grandmother will die
not caring what happened
to the gold that embraced that woman's feet.
My father will die
trying to tell me things he regrets
no one cared to remember.
He will tell me his dreams,
share small stories he thinks someone may have told him.
I will die chanting the songs my Mothers taught me.
Their voices will be heard.

M. Eliza Hamilton

Cornelius Eady   Rita Dove

I Just Wanna Testify

There was, at the end, a look of great peace on my
father's face at the moment of his death. At the
memorial service my cousin tells this story to us as
a way to infer a last-minute salvation, a meeting of
Jesus in the middle of the air, this being, after all, the
AME Zionist church across from the vacant lot that
used to be the elementary school.

This is the part of the service where we stand up
for him, this small knot of family and friends in a very
large room.

He's gone and left my mother with nothing. Her
name isn't on the deed to the house, her name never
appears on his policies. Her mind's confused, she
can't take care of herself by herself, and I'm having
a real hard time convincing various agencies that she
even exists.

Which is why there is no casket to bear. Too
expensive, we decide, money to be better spent on
the living, on my mother.

Still, we give him a family send-off. *A hard man,
but his own man!* sing the testimonies. *A stingy man,
but a family man!* And I truthfully thank him for
the roof he put over our heads, for staying when a
lot of other men took a look at their wives, their
babies, their house bills and changed their names
to fare-thee-well.

And then my sister stands up, stands up through
the pain and accidents of first born, first torn, stands
up, the family's "bad girl," the willful daughter,
low-down spirit of red dresses and iodine, my sister
stands up in a way I can't fully explain, but know
belongs to black women, she stands up and declares,
*I'm just like him, but I'm a woman, so I can't get away
with it.*

Cornelius Eady

Anti-Father

Contrary to
tales you told us

summer nights when
the air conditioner

broke—the stars
are not far

apart. Rather
they draw

closer together
with years.

And houses
shrivel, un-lost,

and porches sag;
neighbors phone

to report cracks
in the cellar floor

roots of the willow
coming up. Stars

speak to a child.
The past

is silent . . .
Just between

me and you,
woman to man,

outer space is
inconceivably

intimate.

Rita Dove

Foreign Exchange

 *Edward Hirsch* *Anna Swir*

The Skokie Theatre

Twelve years old and lovesick, bumbling
and terrified for the first time in my life,
but strangely hopeful, too, and stunned,
definitely stunned—I wanted to cry,
I almost started to sob when Chris Klein
actually touched me—oh God—below the belt
in the back row of the Skokie Theatre.
Our knees bumped helplessly, our mouths
were glued together like flypaper, our lips
were grinding in a hysterical grimace
while the most handsome man in the world
twitched his hips on the flickering screen
and the girls began to scream in the dark.
I didn't know one thing about the body yet,
about the deep foam filling my bones,
but I wanted to cry out in desolation
when she touched me again, when the lights
flooded on in the crowded theatre
and the other kids started to file
into the narrow aisles, into a lobby
of faded purple splendor, into the last
Saturday in August before she moved away.
I never wanted to move again, but suddenly
we were being lifted toward the sidewalk
in a crush of bodies, blinking, shy,
unprepared for the ringing familiar voices

and the harsh glare of sunlight, the brightness
of an afternoon that left us gripping
each other's hands, trembling and changed.

Edward Hirsch

The Youngest Children of an Angel

When you kissed me for the first time
we became a couple
of the youngest children of an angel,
which just started
to fledge.

Lapsed into a silence in mid-move,
hushed in mid-breath,
astounded
to the very blood,
they listen with their bodies
to the sprouting on their shoulder blades
of the first little plume.

Anna Swir
Translated by Czeslaw Milosz with Leonard Nathan

Philip Booth   *Marion Winik*

He

He was fifteen. And she, Wisconsin:
rolling, vernal, a fern to the sun
who answered her green question mark.

There were fields beyond them: clover
and buttercup, paintbrush, lupin;
daisy and daisy, over and over,

under bobolink, goldfinch, and lark.
He laughed out like a jack-in-the-pulpit,
woken up from the difficult dark.

Philip Booth

Foreign Exchange

I used to think you could get a boy
to kiss you by telepathy
if you could think it hard enough
that a bolt of blue desire
would jump jagged from your brain
to his.

Then I heard you have to get him
alone, take him outside, look into his eye,
then the other eye, then both eyes at once.

Now I'm told that to get something
I have to give up wanting it.
This I will never understand.
What's the use of a kiss you don't want
any more?

How can a person make herself go to work,
drive the car, wash her hair, change her
clothes, get up, sit down, get up again,
and so on, without a kiss to break up
the monotony? Sometimes it's impossible to go on
without a kiss, as if your life were a run-on
sentence, as if your life were the Berlin Wall
with soldiers guarding your openings,
as if there were not enough mouths
to go around in the village, and your lips
were swollen with hunger
scrabbling with your sisters for one dried-up
kiss the size of a silver dollar.

Marion Winik

 Gary Hyland   Diana O'Hehir

Fet Walks Melody Home

Is she too quiet or am I
swamping her with jabber?
In Budapest students
our age battle tanks.
I chuck snowballs at trees,
worry that my coat's too small.
Oh, I love her furry boots.
Didja see the show at the Cap?

Yeah, Elaine and I went last night.
Should I talk more or does he
prefer good listeners?
He asks questions then clams up.
Looks like a kid in that coat
and clowns like one in the snow.
Wish he was more mature.
Why'd I wear these stupid boots?

Gary Hyland

Questions and Answers

Who'll marry me? Cold Saturday. *Will he leave me?* With the
        blinds half pulled. *How will I*
Love him? Hastily. Now,
Can you finish your trip before dark?

You must go by the top of the hill, the bus, the bridge, the hedge,
        the bench,
There you'll be a child,
Your scrawny arms together,
Your hands clutching a pocketbook. You have a dime and a
        nickel. You're going
Down the road, across the town,
To the school, the store; you'll dance once across the supermarket
        parking lot,
Flare like a lighted pinecone,
Fade dull gray.

And there your coffin will be waiting, old lady.
Row it home
With your own two hands.

Now who'll marry me?
The green man with eyelashes of corn silk, the tall boy with the
        dripping wet hair,
The lover with a valley full of wheat.

Diana O'Hehir

Paul Bonin-Rodriguez   *Judith Barrington*

Steven Pudenz

I've kept a place for Steven Pudenz
All semester on this bus,
He's two stops down—
A world away!—

(He gets on with wet hair, just from the shower, pushing it
behind his ears . . .)

Past the Talavera's and Beck's
Ten savages in all.
My eyes averted, my books next to me
Tell them like hell you'll sit here.

He's got a few word way of saying a lot
"I dunno" means it's not worth thinking about
"Didn't read it, forgot" means there were more pressing concerns
He's briefly honest

(He returns as wet at the end of the day, after athletics . . .)

When we finally pull up to Pudenz Ranch
I briefly glance around, then shift,
As if the bus's movement has pushed me aside,
And prepare myself to translate, "This seat taken?"

(Do you want a best friend? What are you doing the rest of your
life? Prom?)

I've kept a place for Steven Pudenz
For six months on this bus.
And for all but one of those days,
His sister has taken the seat.

(I'm getting a car and running her down.)

Paul Bonin-Rodriguez

Dirty Panes

Down by the greenhouse
her friends were discussing boys.
The dull pop of a ball
from the courts beyond
kissed the air
like the plump burps of the frogs
that bobbed up and down
through the slime on the lily pond.

Down by the greenhouse Lottie was telling all:
his hands and where they went,
his scratchy face.
The one on the edge of the group
examined the wall—
the curve of each rounded pebble
each folded crevice.

Inside the greenhouse,
strictly out of bounds,
Lottie was telling them
all about french kissing:
the tongue . . . the lips . . . like this . . .
she grabbed at Rose
and kissed her full on the mouth,
bodies pressing.

Condensation ran down
the dirty panes
as the dyke with no name
sucked in the steamy air.
She tried to laugh like her friends
but her mouth was locked
to hold in the words of her heart
that rose like a prayer.

Judith Barrington

 George Bogin   Miriam Kessler

Nineteen

On the first day of Philosophy 148, a small girl walked in,
freckled, solemn, cute, whom I liked right off.

Next time, our eyes met and she smiled a little.
I was already in love.

I always tried to arrive before she did so I could watch her
coming through the doorway, each time loving her more.

She began to look at me, too, hoping for a word, I suppose,
but when our eyes met mine would drop.

Once I heard her ask someone for a pencil.
I passed mine back without turning or speaking.

Spring came and we saw each other on the campus
open-throated, wordless, everywhere.

On the last day of exam week I was reading at the far end
of the Philosophy Library. Not a soul there but the librarian.
Dust in the sunbeams. End of college.

The door opened. It was my girl. I looked down.

In all that empty library she came to my side,
to the very next chair. Sweet springtime love.
Lovely last chance first love.

I could have taken her by the hand and walked the whole 60 blocks
to the piers right onto a steamer to France or somewhere,
but I said nothing and after a while got up
and walked out into middle age.

George Bogin

All Their Names Were Vincent

All their names were Vincent, Ernie, Paul,
black-haired, blue-eyed, splinter-thin.
Their legs were lanky.
They were shod in smooth black leather.
They did not love me . . .
loved Elsie, Margaret, Mary.
Only Elmers, Horaces and Walts loved me.
They had faded-ocean eyes
and less than blond limp hair,
the kind that balds at twenty,
chins that melt into the throat,
sans muscle, sinew, tendon, bone.
All their voices rasped
like grain against rough board.
Their breath was hot and wheezy,
smelled of onion. It was raw
in morning classrooms where,
unlike Margaret, Mary, Elsie,
I excelled in English
and I let it show.
Where Miss Campbell always caught me
talking out of turn
and said **Detention!**

Where are Vincent, Ernie, Paul?
I do not miss them now.
I married Pete.
We are each other's more than thirty years.
The time swims past like barracudas

snapping at the days.
We are each other's
and the breath of onion,
grain against rough board,
and even psuedo-English-accented Miss Campbell
vanish into vapor
and are gone.

Miriam Kessler

 Charles Simic *Nora Mitchell*

The Inner Man

It isn't the body
That's a stranger.
It's someone else.

We poke the same
Ugly mug
At the world.
When I scratch,
He scratches too.

There are women
Who claim to have held him.
A dog follows me about.
It might be his.

If I'm quiet, he's quieter.
So I forget him.
Yet, as I bend down
To tie my shoelaces,
He's standing up.

We cast a single shadow.
Whose shadow?

I'd like to say:
"He was in the beginning
And he'll be in the end,"
But one can't be sure.

At night
As I sit
Shuffling the cards of our silence,
I say to him:

"Though you utter
Every one of my words,
You are a stranger.
It's time you spoke."

Charles Simic

The Locker Room

Everywhere else we wrapped our bodies
tight in corduroy, down, and wool,

but there we took our clothes off
and walked about in the humid
sweaty warmth with its faint sting
of chlorine. At first,
eighteen, a bit shocked
and shy, I carried my towel
in front of me to the showers,
not quite willing
to go covered or uncovered.
There was always some naked woman
walking from the sauna to her locker,
matter of fact, as if she were out
running an errand, though I never saw
those women buying perfume
or Tampax, or crossing campus
with their files and books.
Coming in from the stiff cold
of January and of the men who did not want us
in their college, we crossed
a glassed-in bridge above the two blue pools
where the men's team practiced, their clean
thin bodies plying between the walls
on a bead above the black racing lines.
Inside the door of our locker room
heat knocked us woozy,
as we started to strip down.

Nora Mitchell

 *Gevorg Emin*   *Mary Clark*

In the Orchard

In the orchard at twilight
as the trees fall asleep
I'm picking cherries
from the smallest of trees.

In the dusk the tree trembles
as if it is being disrobed,

and I feel as it shivers
as if I'm slipping off
the jewels from the ears
of my little love.

Gevorg Emin
Translated by Diana Der Hovanessian

Summer, At Home

The goats were still
until dark.
The sheep stood
in the strip of shade
by the wall.
The figs hung, full
and weighty.

After they dropped,
flourescent insects covered
their pink insides.
When we hated each other enough,
we wrestled on the lawn.
The grass made our skin itch.
That night, I wanted you
the way I wanted you.
I sat at the table eating
one fig after another,
asking you, come here,
if you love me, get sick
on these with me.

Mary Clark

 Cornelius Eady   Nellie Wong

January

The old man wants to dance
But can't get started.
May I dance with you? Not yet,
Laughs the beautiful girl
As she spins away
In an air-light
Dress.

He'll never catch up.
It's written right here in the script.
It has something to do
With the balance of the world.

If he catches her,
What will he lose?
The general feeling
That some ideals
Are impossible to live with.

But it will go harder on us.
It will be another thing
We can't just quite put our fingers on,
A slight feeling
Of uneasiness,

Something about the color of the sky,
An alien texture to the air.

The old man wants to dance.
Here are the hard facts:
She'll always be
A few steps ahead of him.

Not yet, she laughs.
Pursuing her,
The other months bounce along behind
Like cans
Tied to the honeymoon bumper.

Cornelius Eady

Where Are You Going?

Where are you going now?
Why don't you stay home
and clean the house?

How will you learn
to catch
a husband
if you do nothing on Saturdays
but hang out
at the beauty parlor
then shop all day
to adorn your body?

Why don't you
watch me
cook rice
wash windows
scrub floors
darn sox?

Why don't you?

I am only your mother
I am getting old
Don't you see these white hairs?

Soon I will be in my grave
and even if you get married
and even if you get married

and bear me a grandson
and bear me a grandson
it will have the name, the name, the name
of a stranger,
stranger,
stranger.

Nellie Wong

  Conrad Hilberry   Nina Cassian

Spoon

I'm the short one, the empty face
collecting all the other faces.
My only talent is to play
Sweet Afton on some water glasses

or make a friendly racket to
back up the banjo. I'm what old-
time lovers do with moonlight and how
three children in a bed may fold

their knees together to keep warm.
The fork holds down the chicken while
the knife cuts leg from thigh, breast meat
from bone. I recognize their style,

but I work alone. Tonight, I'll slip
into the bowl and lift hot soup to your lip.

Conrad Hilberry

Equality

If I dress up like a peacock,
you dress like a kangaroo.
If I make myself into a triangle,
you acquire the shape of an egg.
If I were to climb on water,
you'd climb on mirrors.

All our gestures
belong to the solar system.

Nina Cassian
Translated by Brenda Walker with the poet

 Albert Goldbarth   Tess Gallagher

Hey Sweetie

The things we call women! housewife, honey,
whore. The things we call the night: O
Mother of Terrors. Soft, Black, Velvet
Horse's Nostril I Worm Through. Braille

Rainbows Under The Blanket. Names telling
more about the namer.

*

Often as a child I needed a star
to fall to sleep by. A dimestore "night light"
in the shape of a fish. A Flash Gordon Glow-In-The-Dark Ring.
Or: the years my sister shared my room
I told her a bedroom story each night—the
dependency of binary stars.

*

Well it *is* night, and somebody's called for.
What the iced-up bowel of fear does to a businessman
flying, I have no right to guess. But he's
blanched and sweating. And she's a figure, really,
between wings. There's a stew light. In the dark he calls her
angel and who's to say he's not right.

Albert Goldbarth

Conversation with a Fireman from Brooklyn

He offers, between planes,
to buy me a drink. I've never talked
to a fireman before, not one from Brooklyn
anyway. Okay. Fine, I say. Somehow
the subject is bound to come up, women
firefighters, and since I'm
a woman and he's a fireman, between
the two of us, we know something
about this subject. Already

he's telling me he doesn't mind
women firefighters, but what
they look like
after fighting a fire, well
they lose all respect. He's sorry, but
he looks at them
covered with the cinders of someone's
lost hope, and he feels disgust, he just
wants to turn the hose on them, they
are that sweaty and stinking, just like
him, of course, but not the woman he
wants, you get me? and to come to that—
isn't it too bad, to be despised
for what you do to prove yourself
among men
who want to love you, to love you,
love you.

Tess Gallagher

 *Kim Stafford*   *Pamela Alexander*

Proposal

The sign for our town
has fallen off the road
into the field.
Wheat gives with the wind.

Bending, the stalks drop seed.
The bearded ears of winter
wheat have their own
whispered song. May our
town's defeat be graceful.

Past where the edge of town was,
sit in the wheat and ask
a friend her name. Rain
is coming; don't get up.

Kim Stafford

Fish Fact

for Carolyn

Two fish
alive, strangely, in air
lay fat and heavy,
one in my hands and one in yours,
and looked peaceful,
happy, even.
We hadn't caught them;
shiny and solid,
they materialized
as we sat in the dinghy
in a harbor
under the wide sun,
looking at each other,
good friends.

What I remember
after falling up the familiar darkness
that always surprises
at the end of sleep
is that they were different:
yours had stripes
and mine was mottled.
So the meaning that follows me
above the surface of sleep
(the meaning, always less
than the dream)
is that we are different,
in the middle of all we share, and that
we can be peaceful with that fact,
happy, even, in our strangely
shining lives.

Pamela Alexander

 Ronald Koertge   Grace Paley

The Ubiquity of the Need for Love

I leave the number and a short
message on every green Volvo
in town

    Is anything wrong?
    I miss you.
    574-7423

The phone rings constantly.
One says, Are you bald?
Another, How tall are you in
your stocking feet?

Most just reply, Nothing's wrong.
I miss you, too.

Come quick.

Ronald Koertge

Love

Handsome men wearing red ties walk past my window
not one but three   this morning!   their coats open
their ties flying   as though spring had made some
deliberate move on our street   maybe a fur-tipped
bud among the hedges   a fact: years and
years ago I saw you pass   your face rosy from that
interior lifelong commotion   your head forward
stubborn against a March wind   day after day
for nearly a month   as you walked with considerable eagerness toward your daily life
right past my window   I thought   who
is that man   then I thought oh
I already know him

Grace Paley

 David Clewell   Nina Cassian

Goodbye Note to Debbie Fuller: Pass It On

Whoever this Debbie Fuller is in your poems,
she ought to be collecting royalties.

—a loyal reader

When we passed those notes to each other and laughed
behind Miss Jago's back in Hamilton School, we were flirting
with real danger. The secret insults and atonement
that passed for our friendship seemed effortless in cursive,
too easily could have become a part of our Permanent Record.
Those days we got away with more than we ever imagined,
so many ways of saying I'm sorry again, I won't do it
anymore, and I promise not to get you
into trouble from now on. As if we could help ourselves.

If I've named names under pressure in my life since then
in the late-night interrogation rooms of the heart,
if I've had to write out one more doctored confession,
give up on maintaining my innocence one more night
and your name is the one I keep coming back to,
I'll admit it: you're the alibi I've needed, the only one
who can place me miles and years away from the dried blood,
the chalked outline of childhood on the sidewalk. Otherwise
I'm looking at some serious hard time, and you know
I'll be taking you with me.

Say I fell hard for those dirty blonde bangs, those doleful eyes,
those corduroy skirts and OK, finally, even the way you moved
to Basking Ridge, New Jersey that December of '65
without breathing a word to anyone, not even to me
in the holiday assembly when I was the top of the wobbling
human Christmas tree and you placed that cardboard star on my head
with a kiss we never practiced in rehearsal.
How could you know what you were lighting up forever,
improvising one last piece of business that was nowhere
in the script? Maybe no one told you either,
or you didn't know how to say it. Maybe that day was
your rendition of uncanny grace under pressure.
I was ten and thought I knew everything
I could possibly want for Christmas for the rest of my life.

I wanted you earlier in the alphabet, or taller, depending
on any given day's meticulous instructions for lining up
on our way to whatever came next. My faintest hope was always
rained-out gym, huddled inside, boy-girl-boy-
girl for almost an hour, no questions asked. God, I wanted you
to realize how much it mattered too. Those were the days
before love knew its own name, almost before hormones
in their nervous skirmishes at the borders of wherever we were.

I don't know why, after so many years of everything
I've put you through in words—silent partner
in a thousand schemes, or worse, my unwitting accomplice—
you still keep coming back to me. As if it's been in your power
to refuse, as if you've had anything to say. I'll confess again:
I've used you, but I guess I'd like to think I haven't
used you up completely. So here's my promise at long last:

you won't have to get dressed on short notice, hurry out of a house
full of people who love you more for whatever you've become.
No more questions of *what do I wear* in this poem, *what
can he possibly want from me now?* I'll leave you alone
to look me up in your own quiet version of time.

And people who insist on reading this before it gets to you
can sigh and shake their heads if they want to, as long
as they keep it moving while the world drones on
through its baffling arithmetic, geography without end,
through its far-flung chalky sense of history
while the radiators hiss and the clock lops off another minute
you're too far away to whisper all this in your ear.
As long as they know this one's for Debbie Fuller,
for old times' sake, for all the good it does,
from the kid still making any promise he can get away with:
it won't happen again, I swear,
or your name's not Debbie Fuller. Debbie Fuller,
it won't ever happen again.

David Clewell

Performances

He overtook a cruiser in a tiny boat.
He burst through a window without breaking it.
He jumped in the street with one sock tied to the other.
He claimed to have eight dads yet no mother.

He unscrewed mountains. He licked pollen,
He boasted the exact number of nerves in a cat.
Always elated, never sullen,
he knew he deserves all he gets.

He was even capable of packing a carpet in a
                                        very small tube.

So she fell in love with him—heard wedding bells!

But then his ego began to sneeze.
And apart from sneezing
he couldn't do much else.

Nina Cassian
Translated by Brenda Walker with the poet

  Jack Gilbert   Harryette Mullen

Meaning Well

Marrying is like somebody
throwing the baby up.
It happy and them throwing it
higher. To the ceiling.
Which jars the loose bulb
and it goes out
as the baby starts down.

Jack Gilbert

Jump City

I feel a little jumpy around you.
Like when I think a house has
roaches, and I watch everything
out the corner of my eye to see
if it crawls away.

Harryette Mullen

 *Peter Oresick* *Grace Paley*

The Passion and Woe in Marriage: A Ukrainian Love Story

She came to America with him
because of his "such curly-nice
black hair."
The way he cocks his head,
the way he chews his words,
are still amusing, she thinks.
She says she can balance pop bottles
    on his lower lip.

Their passion is so great
they have been glancing secretly
at each other for forty-six years
while tending shop.
She tells him she would break his nose
but she only has two hands.

She tells him she should have married
her intellectual third cousin from Kiev,
the priest's son,
as she goes to straighten the stacks of corduroy.

Both realize how important spirituality is:
he dreams he rides the steppes
a proud son of Abraham with saber and yarmulkah;
she dreams her novenas strike him down.

Peter Oresick

Quarrel

Bob and I
      in different rooms
      talking to ourselves
carrying on
      last night's
      hard conversation
convinced
      the other one
      the life companion
      wasn't listening

Grace Paley

 *Gevorg Emin* *Anne Waldman*

Your Hands

I love your hands
which hold me,
held me,
for so many years
without
binding me,

hands which make
me master
without mastering me,

encircle
without
strangling me,

lift me
the way the drowning
man is lifted,

hands
whose cupped shells
change me

slowly slowly
into the pearl
they wanted
all the time.

Gevorg Emin
Translated by Diana Der Hovanessian

Two Men

Writing to one man of another. Now there are 2 &
I am writing of them. I write to one of them. I
write to one of them of the other one. Heart &
muscles and toes of men. Arms & legs & ears of men.
They are listening to hear about each other, one
to hear about the other one. I write of them.
I wrote to them. I write to one of them of the
other one. I write to him. I write to them.
They don't want to hear it. Writing of them.
Writing of them. They are next to one another
in my writing, now they are separated by my
writing. They might hate one another by my
writing. It could be romantic writing of them
to them. They look out different windows. They
hold me in common arms. I write to them. Is
it fair? Writing to one man of another one?
I write of them. I am writing of them & to them so
as you know me so they know me. I tell the truth.

Eyes & mouths & fingers of men. 2 of them. I'm
not a wicked woman, I am writing of them. It
is harmless. Knees of men. It is harmless.
Thighs of men. It does not change anything.

Anne Waldman

William Virgil Davis   Christianne Balk

January

One morning I awoke and found that it had been snowing all
night inside my body. The snow was still falling, filtering down
through my ribs, filling in my arms and legs. Already my feet
were full. In the left leg the snow was as deep as the knee, as if I
had stepped into a hole.

Then I could no longer move. My legs were too heavy, weighted
with the snow. When I tried to speak I found my tongue swollen,
my mouth frozen shut. It was only January and I had promised
to visit a young woman who lived alone in one room above a
garage. She had long black hair and never laughed. She must be
wondering what happened to me.

William Virgil Davis

The Yellow Hills in Back

I can't tell my husband about the vacant lot
below my fourth floor window, in back
of the Mercy Hospital parking ramp.
Where all the city streets end.
The ground is pale, fawn-brown, and hard—
cracked like a man-made lake bank
cracks before the crown vetch and pampas grass
take root. We talk about his truck. The weather.
Then his truck again. I don't want to talk
about the child I lost two days ago, the second
child I've lost. His children. When I look
at him he looks straight past me, looks
at the wall. As if he were looking down the westbound
lane of Interstate 80 north of Lincoln, Nebraska.
Nowhere near this town. I stare outside
at the trefoil-covered hills south of town,
hills heaped like mounds of sulfur, hills
that slowly blend into the chlorine-colored pastures.
Black cows graze out there. Their calves lie still.
Outside, the catalpa leaves sway and throw
netted shadows on the streets, softening
the edges of the cinder block houses.
The silence settles down on both of us
like a sheet draped on two living room chairs
in a cottage by a lake in late October.

Christianne Balk

Gunnar Ekelöf   *Joan Logghe*

For Night Comes

For night comes
when happiness and unhappiness
rest in peace with each other

You see how quickly the dusk falls
like belltolls
and window after window lights up

Inside there they have eaten their spaghetti
and without a thought of the coming day
they will soon sleep next to each other

For the night comes:
No next day exists:
No city exists

Gunnar Ekelöf
Translated by Robert Bly

Marriage

Sometimes in the evening,
in the hot evening, sometimes Sophia
and Manny drive into town.
They park at the Sonic Drive-in
facing north. There's a green lawn
and some elms across the way.

We can pretend, she says,
that we're in the mountains.
It's cool here. The roof
is full of birds, I can hear them
but I can't see what kind.

They get two-for-one Cokes
and sit together in the truck, close.
Sophia takes Manny's hand,
he's not the type in public.
It's just summer. Sophia
takes ice and rubs some on her face.

They don't have another thing to say.
There's traffic, the birds,
the slurping of soft drinks.
Marriage, the sweet watered down.

Joan Logghe

 William Pitt Root   Toi Derricotte

Estrangements

A man and his wife are estranged.

They have a child
they love.

The child returns from a visit
with the father
carrying a sack of candy
the mother sees and takes
and throws away.

The child cries, the mother cries,
the father, if he knew,
would cry.

The father knows.
His wife has told him
of that illness, often.
How the hands chill,
the eyes glaze.

But the father loves the child
and the child loves the father.
Neither has a full knowledge of love
and there are things
to be put in love's place.

So the child cries, the mother cries,
and the father, if he knew,
would cry.

William Pitt Root

The Friendship

I tell you I am angry.
You say you are afraid.
You take your glasses off and lay
them on the table like a sparkling weapon.
I hold my purse in front of me.
Do I love you? Do you love me?
"If we just had time . . ."

You could show me how you wore your hair
pushed forward over one eye, hiding
half of what you knew of beauty.

Poor friendship, why must it sit
at a table where the waitress
is ready to go home? In a city
between tunnels—cracks
of darkness in the sea.

Toi Derricotte

 **Hugo Williams**   *Yaedi Ignatow*

Gone Away

We leave each other and the habits
Fall away like sight of land.

Now I am featureless
And you are infinite again.

Hugo Williams

We Were Love

We were love
or love was suddenly remembering us
the way two lines cross
and the nearest necessity
you know nothing about, finds you.
The way two people meeting
can suddenly slice through the fabric of an evening
revealing the fabric of another evening in another world.
The way
we don't have to know everything;
we just have to want to let everything know us.

Yaedi Ignatow

E. Ethelbert Miller   Naomi Stroud Simmons

Dressed Up

one day
i'm gonna
be dressed
up in a coffin

have a nice
tie and suit
on

my old
girlfriend
won't have
to complain
about me
wearing jeans
every place
i go

one day
when i'm
dressed up
in my coffin

i'm gonna
ask her out

take her
somewhere
she hasn't
been

E. Ethelbert Miller

With Reservations

He preens his plumes while strutting proud,
determined to impress her.
He is the darling of the crowd
that dashing fancy dresser.
But she can always change his tune
and minor key his song.
She will concede he hung the moon,
but says he hung it wrong.

Naomi Stroud Simmons

Ronald Wallace   Anna Swir

The Real Thing

The sea was as blue as the sky
and your eyes were as blue as the sea.
Could I help it?
I was happy. We were in love.

And the jellyfish floating in on the tide?
And the gulls in their lovely remoteness?
Who could see through
the blue angle of their descent,
the accuracy of stinger and beak,
the sea in its cool movement,
swelling? Who could care?

Oh the sky was our limitless future,
and the rhythmic sea laving the beach
was our love going on, and forever.
Could I help it?

And the bright starfish trapped in the shallows?
And the sea urchins reft of their spines?
And the shells with their ears full of memories?
Who could care? We were young;
how could summer and language betray us,
leave us stranded in this blue season,
our tongues blunt as husks in our cheeks?

Ronald Wallace

Astonishment

I have been looking at you
for so many years
that you have become perfectly invisible.
But I did not realize it yet.

Yesterday
by chance I exchanged kisses with someone else.
And only then
I learned with astonishment
that for a long time
you have not been for me a man.

Anna Swir
Translated by Czeslaw Milosz with Leonard Nathan

 Tommy Olofsson   Rhonda Bower

Autobiography

I stem from a tremendous memory.
In the tree's bark I find my face again.
Who can say if this is true or not.

Every person is a mystery, more fantastic
than elves or trolls. This memory
that belongs to no one else but me!

We live with people we don't know. Our best
friends are incredible strangers who live
in different memories. This is what reassures me.

Tommy Olofsson
Translated by Jean Pearson

The Clothespin

Through the window I see
Her, my neighbor.
She hangs his shirt.
It thunders in the breeze.
Clasped by a clothespin
Beside her pale dress.
Side by side, they move.
The clothespin is all
That holds them
together.

Rhonda Bower

Raymond Patterson *Donna Trussell*

Surplus Blues

Everybody gets the blues,
    And I guess I get my share.
Everybody gets the blues, I guess.
    And I guess I get my share.
If I could sell just half of mine
    I'd be a millionaire.

I get the blues in my parlor.
    I get the blues in my kitchen sink.
Sometimes I sit and holler,
    So blue I just can't think.
I get the blues in my bedroom,
    The blues all round my bed,
The blues down in my shoes, Lord,
    And all up in my head.
I get a surplus of blues,
    But the blues ain't in demand.
And nobody wants a blues
    That's second hand.

Raymond Patterson

This Woman

for MLRW

These extra pounds aren't me,
this tired dress,
these vinyl shoes.
I'm not this woman
walking into this house.

      I'm the undeveloped film
      found in the basement.
      I'm the secret pocket in jeans.

No one knows.
My children fight over grapes.
My husband sets his watch.

      I change colors.
      Tonight I'm turquoise
      bleeding into midnight blue.

Donna Trussell

 Robert Long   *Naomi Shihab Nye*

Goodbye

It's a hot day, and I'm sweating
Out the fact that you're gone for good,

That you never loved me
Like I loved you, as the sky
Turns the color of milk: dense, humid,
Halyards clanking a little in the smallest breeze.

All my life I've lived near water:
Rivers around Manhattan, the ocean, bays, and now,
This soggy marina, slathered with sunlight.
Across the uncut lawn,
Through a line of baby spruce,
I can hear the water's slap on fiberglass, wood.

Further off, two egrets fold into marsh grass.
I'm glad you're gone. It gets me
Into my work and out of my mind. I wish
You luck. Out of luck and into myself,
I want to want you somewhere else,
I'd like to not like you as I do.

Slabs of gray cloud unfold:
Air as still as the moment after a yawn.
Boats are quiet: tethered, docked.
Birds start going bananas. Stop it:
It's enough, being here at all, in this same room,
Tide going out, sun going down.

Robert Long

Elevator

We jumped in, trusting
the slow swish of heavy doors,

punching 7, 9, 12.
O swoon of rising stomach! Then a sudden drop.

We took turns popping envelopes into the mail chute
& watching them whiz by from a lower floor.

Where are you? Calling down the tunnel,
sweet high *ding,* nobody's dinnerbell.

In stepped the lady with a fur muff,
her elegant gentleman smelling of New York.

We sobered our faces, bit the glinting arrows
while our father sorted receipts off the lobby.

Goodby! we called to him again & again.
His desk wore a little spike.

Where are you going?
We are going!

Breathing rich perfume & dust
ground into burgundy carpet,

we glistened in the polished edge
of everything that didn't belong to us,

suitcases, humming radios,
brass locks, canisters for ash.

With nowhere to go we became
specialists in Ups & Downs.

Brother! I cried, as he rose to the penthouse without me.
Sister! He wailed as I sank deep into the ground.

Naomi Shihab Nye

 *David Wevill* *Phyllis Janowitz*

Namelessness

By now after all these years
I don't know who the "you" is any more
when the word writes itself instead of a name
or an honest detail. I had forbidden myself
this vagueness, this evasiveness
which is like the shadow that follows this pen
across the page. I had said
honor her memory, or hers, or hers
or speak of the subtle dark one I am with
who asks, what am I to you, am I
nothing?   I have fallen into this habit
of remembering what comes easy to the heart.

You have no name. There is no smell in you
of skin or hair. Your body's word is gone.

David Wevill

Reach

So, she thought, where did he go?
He was just here, he was available,
now he is somewhere, a place like
an island, with a flag in the middle
which must be lowered each night,
and he has a camp-stove, perhaps,
a tent for sleeping and everything
is arranged neatly, as a man alone
arranges things, with an attention
to order that says, "See, see, I am
not mad, I have a name, socks."

And this place, this somewhere,
has no directory. She can not call
him or write. She can only shout
"Come back, come back immediately."
And there—somewhere—he hears
the gulls squawking and scrabbling
over a codfish head, and the soft
swish of water nibbling the shore.

Phyllis Janowitz

The Real Names of Everything

Francisco X. Alarcón   Wendy Barker

Ode to Tomatoes

they make
friends
anywhere

red
smiles
in salads

tender
young
generous

hot
salsa
dancers

round
cardinals
of the kitchen

hard
to imagine
cooking

without
first asking
their blessings!

Francisco X. Alarcón

Canning Season

Tomatoes are rolling
off the vines,

tumbling out of bagfuls
over the kitchen tiles

until we lift them
into the kettle. Simmering,

skins peel off, expose pink
veins tracing over

glistening flesh,
seeds

surrounded in juice
like yolks of tiny eggs.

Sieving out
the pulp

we make sauce,
save August for November.

I hold you now,
We're ripe.

Wendy Barker

 Richard E. McMullen   Fay Lipshitz

It Happens Working

It happens working
on his car alone at night.
His fingers grow longer.
Like wires, they feed deep
into the car's engine,
into its body. They extend,
examine, adjust. They reach
anywhere, touch any
surface. There is no
awkward position. Sometimes
the fingers have eyes, the eyes
night-visioned, comfortable
with heat, with fumes, oil,
gasoline. Sometimes,
briefly, his whole body,
released, goes inside.

Richard E. McMullen

To a Set of Drawing Pencils

Sharp
And straight as infantry
In gray, with scarlet stripe
Bright above insignia
And rank,
From 9B through to F,
Their several heights declare
My preferences.
Tall, untouched, are HB, H and F.
Hard and implacable, unfriendly
To the lie,
Resisting the smudgy finger,
The blurring of what is.
Once, I would have worn
Down to a stub
8 and 9B, for love
Of their velvet dark.
But now, in search of clarity,
Bold, sweet 3B suits my needs.
It blazes across the sheet,
Or leaves
A soft trembling mark.

Fay Lipshitz

 Gary Margolis   Harryette Mullen

For the Woman at the Fast-Food Fish Place Who Called Me Pig

In this place God leaves His morsels unguarded—
crumbs on the breadboard, an extra french fry
left on the cashier's counter, and now the colorful
and extravagant unlocked salad bar I not-so-

innocently graze, waiting for my take-out fish to cook.
Out of the corner of your eye, more than mother-like,
you notice my grazing—I think I am at home—
and turn your fork into a gavel, your raincoat into

a judge's robe. When I feel hungry or guilty, guess
which one wins? My hand floats over the carrot sticks
and bacon bits to the innocent croutons. I know
this franchise boasts nationally its charcoal-broiled

techniques, but the flames I feel are dragon flames,
spewing over me from your unslain booth. Beyond the rhyme,
I'm conscious my snitching *is* uncouth, my hand so
unsanitary you wish the plastic sneeze guard would crash

like a guillotine. The last broccoli spear I take
is the straw that calls your army out, in full chain mail,
visors down, shields up. You march to the teenage
assistant manager and report my deeds by amount

and appetizing category. Handing over my fish and fries,
he looks to me for some assurance that her eyes
will not find a sin of his for condemnation. Seeing
he does not choose or is too young to reprimand

my public cheating, she turns to me and, in a whisper
louder than one God found in His big way to turn
Adam out, she brands me Pig, and sits back down,
with all her ruling knives and forks intact.

Gary Margolis

Momma Sayings

Momma had words for us:
We were "crumb crushers,"
"eating machines,"
"bottomless pits."
Still, she made us charter members
of the bonepickers' club,
saying, "Just don't let your eyes
get bigger than your stomachs."
Saying, "Take all you want,
but eat all you take."
Saying, "I'm not made of money, you know,
and the man at the Safeway
don't give away groceries for free."

She trained us not to leave lights on
"all over the house,"
because "electricity costs money—
so please turn the light off when you leave a room
and take the white man's hand out of my pocket."

When we were small
she called our feet "ant mashers,"
but when we'd outgrow our shoes,
our feet became "platforms."
She told us we must be growing big feet
to support some big heavyset women
(like our grandma Tiddly).

When she had to buy us new underwear
to replace the old ones full of holes,
she'd swear we were growing razor blades in our behinds,
"you tear these drawers up so fast."

Momma had words for us, alright:
She called us "the wrecking crew."
She said our untidy bedroom
looked like "a cyclone struck it."

Our dirty fingernails she called "victory gardens."
And when we'd come in from playing outside
she'd tell us, "You smell like iron rust."
She'd say, "Go take a bath
and get some of that funk off you."
But when the water ran too long in the tub
she'd yell, "That's enough water to wash an elephant."

And after the bath she'd say,
"Be sure and grease those ashy legs."
She'd lemon-cream our elbows
and pull the hot comb
through "these tough kinks on your heads."

Momma had lots of words for us,
her never quite perfect daughters,
the two brown pennies
she wanted to polish
so we'd shine like dimes.

Harryette Mullen

 Khaled Mattawa   Karen Fiser

The Pyramid of Khufu

With each step upward
another was necessary
and every time I looked down
the familiar world seemed
a dangerous place.
I had never intended
to climb to the summit
never thought I could find
refuge in the sky.

The sand below shimmered
until it disappeared
behind a boiling mirage.
With guides, and camels,
the tourists bedecked
in red satin turbans
were like a circus
on a hot plate.
Ten steps down
and I could have heard
faint echoes of their chants.

The world moved slowly
enough for me
to be lost and safe,
enough to be surprised
by what I had already known:
near the tombs of the slaves,
my parents sat
where I left them
in the shade
fanning themselves,
nibbling on pumpkin seeds.

Khaled Mattawa

Wheelchairs That Kneel Down Like Elephants

Last night I rode a tightrope
with my wheelchair. No net.
The night before, I left my body
on the steep ground with its pain.
I walked again by leaning,
elbows careless on the wind,
hitching myself along in light surprise.
Days I am heavy,
a clumsy bear on wheels,
bumping into things
and smiling, smiling. Nights
I invent new means of locomotion:
flying velocipedes, sailcars,
wheelchairs that kneel down
like elephants, carry me carefully
up the long stairs. Intricate
engines of need and night and air.

Karen Fiser

 Agha Shahid Ali   *Cathy Young Czapla*

The Previous Occupant

The landlady says he lived here
for years. There's enough missing
for me to know him. On the empty shelves,

absent books gather dust: Neruda. Cavafy.
I know he knew their poetry, by heart
the lines I love.

From a half-torn horoscope I learn
his sign: Aquarius, just like me.
A half-empty Flexsol in the cabinet:
he wore soft lenses. Yes, Aquarians are vain.
And no anthems on their lips, they travel
great distances. He came from some country
as far as Chile.

She says the apartment
will be cleaned by the 1st:

But no detergent will rub his voice from the air
though he has disappeared in some country
as far as Chile.
The stains of his thoughts still cling
in phrases to the frost on the windows.

And though he is blinded in some prison,
though he is dying in some country
as far as Chile,
no spray will get inside the mirror
from where his brown eyes,
brown, yes, brown,
stare as if for years he'd been
searching for me.

Now that he's found me,
my body casts his shadow everywhere.
He'll never, never, move out of here.

Agha Shahid Ali

Carpenter's Daughter

I always woke to
bedrooms marked off with masking tape and
the smell of joint compound mixed with mountain
air. The tools all knew their proper names—
blue chalk-line, straight-claw hammer, level,
steel tape, combination square and bench vise.
I learned to respect the circular saw and
the man—the power behind it. I learned
all the textures of sawdust.
I learned my mother's fears—
falling ladders,
slippery roofs,
the momentary lapse in attention that
took off the tip of one finger,

the storm
when lightning scratched blue lines
through falling snow, and the wind
picked up the sheetmetal roofing
and carried it over my father's head.

Cathy Young Czapla

Gregory Orfalea   *Faye Kicknosway*

War

And so it begins in play
with the splashing in a small pool
and the shriek at errant water
in the eye, or legs swelling
with adrenaline to run and leap.
Soon they are in a heap. And the elder
pushes the younger who has the audacity
to be there. He stares at first deeply
before crying at his brother as if
for the first time. They were one
breath of air, and now two. It is
not long before the elder has a scar
to show he is not the only one wrong.
The day and night join—see the red
pulled like seared flesh far off?
They run. They laugh and grow
and destroy. I can't stop it.
I know what happens to boys.

Gregory Orfalea

West Grand Boulevard

Three small children,
impatient at the bus stop,
practice karate:

a toe to the kidney,
to the throat.
Their mother, her arms full
of packages, watches them.
She's going to give them
something more old-fashioned
when they get home.

Faye Kicknosway

Gerald Stern   Joan Fern Shaw

Cow Worship

I love the cows best when they are a few feet away
from my dining-room window and my pine floor,
when they reach in to kiss me with their wet
mouths and their white noses.
I love them when they walk over the garbage cans
and across the cellar doors,
over the sidewalk and through the metal chairs
and the birdseed.
—Let me reach out through the thin curtains
and feel the warm air of May.
It is the temperature of the whole galaxy,
all the bright clouds and clusters,
beasts and heroes,
glittering singers and isolated thinkers
at pasture.

Gerald Stern

Cow

Chewing cud
homely
big tongue
sliding
into nostrils
big eyes
watching me
with apathy

But I was young
and eager to love

I threw my thin white
city arms around her neck
She stopped chewing
then resumed
without breaking
jaw-stride

But I was young
and used to indifference

Joan Fern Shaw

 *Geof Hewitt*   *Karen Fiser*

Typographical Errors

Don't let them bother you, she said.
After all, those are just worlds.

Geof Hewitt

Teaching Myself to Read

From the first only saying
made things real. I climbed up word
for word the cliff face of all
four-year-old sorrows, reading
the signs in a heavy sky:
PABST. JAX. COKE. The marvel
was that these big neon signs
(unlike the small signs of home
trouble brewing) could be read.
I'd drag my father's heavy
books down to the floor and hold
Last Man Off Wake Island close
to my eyes for hours. Inching
my finger across magic
black rows, I longed to unlock
that secret syntax and just
read myself out of this world.

Karen Fiser

 Eric Nelson   Christine Hemp

Kitchens

Most open of rooms,
only here do you find
no mirrors.

The way some men
remember women,
I remember kitchens:
the smells and warmth,
the sweet hidden things,
the ghosts of mothers.

I may have been born
in one, like a kitten,
beneath the sink in the dark,
lemon oil over me.

Before the slow
spread of dawnlight, the flash
of kitchen windows.
Before the even flow,
the startling clang
of pipes, storm of water.

Any decisions that count
are made here, delicate
as dishes, final as knives.

Coffee steams a fine line
toward the smoke alarm.

On the refrigerator door,
messages and menus,
postcards and comics,
emergency numbers. Haphazard
pictures of ourselves
open and shut.

Eric Nelson

Living Lean

I move through houses like a hermit crab.
The chair tells me to get up.
The windows want privacy.
The landlady wants me gone.

I'm tired
of all this packing up of pans and spoons,
of matters of the heart.

I dream of apricots,
orchards by a stream,
the sound of a clothesdryer,
the slam of a screen door.

Christine Hemp

Jacinto Jesús Cardona   *Sandra M. Gilbert*

The Old Dream Oven

Father is the number one small town fry cook,
walking home from the late shift
at the Palace Grille on Highway 281,
escorted by a line of cats, stray cats
smelling the salmon croquettes,
the jumbo shrimp that slept in the Gulf
just last night.

Yes, Father is the number one
small town fry cook,
coming home on calloused feet,
lugging a bucketful of day-old doughnuts.

But on cold December mornings,
he rises early, rolls up a newspaper,
strikes a match, and lights up
the old dream oven.

He is going to make pancakes,
he is going to make the perfect pancake,
he is going after the big one,
the one that always gets away,
the ultimate pancake.

Without a mixer,
he whips up the batter,

Just like a hall of fame kitchen jock,
he cannot stop.

He makes stacks and stacks of pancakes.
Despierten! ya'stan listos los pancakes! *
Come and get 'em,
they're going like hotcakes.

Jacinto Jesús Cardona

* Get up! The pancakes are already ready!

The Dream Kitchen

Her eyes glowed pale as radium.
She said: "Well, if you're good
I'll let you come into
the dream kitchen . . ."

I was demure. Plaid skirt,
white anklets, gold barrette,
clasped hands always before me
like the hands of the dead.

She said: "Well?"
                        and I followed her
through the tall door,
and the dream kitchen

with its pulsing ovens
rose around us like a mountain range,
the dream kitchen held us in fleshy
silence, the dream kitchen

rocked us, stroked us,
streaming with syrups and creams
and soupy hollows.
"Check out the cupboards,"

she said. "Open the drawers.
The place is all yours."
I pulled a throbbing handle: streaks of cutlery.
Another: platters inscribed "I'm yours."

"Remember your manners."
I turned to thank her,
but she was gone:
I was alone.

My enormous kitchen coughed, trembled,
and began to hum.

Sandra M. Gilbert

 Jim Wayne Miller   Marylee Skwirz

A Plague of Telephones

They infest my life.
Attaching themselves to walls, they sit
like locusts clutching treebark
in a seventeenth summer.
Silence is the scratching
of their feet on scattered papers.
They crawl on me, creep into my ears
and cling there, bulging with bad news, singing
Pharaoh, Pharaoh!

Jim Wayne Miller

Long Distance Calls

With my oldest son, I talk
of cats. These
we have shared.
He tells me of the well-being
of his, inquires about mine.
Our behavior in regard to cats is always
correct, compassionate, honorable. No
recriminations on either side. We approve
each other's cats.

The small talk does not
include his wife, my daughters—his sisters.

And the little cats?
They do not cry.

Marylee Skwirz

 Zbigniew Herbert   *Ingrid Wendt*

Mother

He fell from her knees like a ball of yarn.
He unwound in a hurry and ran blindly away.
She held the beginning of life. She would wind it
on her finger like a ring, she wanted to preserve him.
He was rolling down steep slopes, sometimes
he was climbing up. He would come back tangled, and be silent.
Never will he return to the sweet throne of her knees.

The stretched-out hands are alight in the darkness
like an old town.

Zbigniew Herbert
Translated by John Carpenter and Bogdana Carpenter

The Teacher I Wanted to Be

my own forever, my mother
asked home to lunch each spring,

each spring someone new:
Miss Bloss, Mrs. Kuk, Miss Michaelson never
suspecting we waited for blossom time,

hoping the rain would hold off long enough,
counting the days like notes of that year's recital piece
always I played for her, practicing

hours longer than any
hundred years' sleep any child could ever imagine:
the princess, the castle awakening, parting

branches blossoming over that aisle of tulips and lilacs, bright
promises I didn't know I was making someday
to become that same teacher each spring

on the last day of school surprised by a girl planting
instead of a secret next to the ear bent low
a kiss, so quick she never could hear what running

all the way home, crying, she all year
had listened for: yes, she was
yes, a good girl

a good
girl
a good girl.

Ingrid Wendt

 Albert Huffstickler   *Rosemary Catacalos*

Lament for an Old Woman

She has gone to the valley.
She has taken the long walk.
She has wrapped herself in a bundle of weariness
and trudged off toward the high mountains.
She has wrapped some biscuits in a blue bandanna
and will not be back for supper.

She has gone to the valley.
She has measured her last cup of flour.
She has rolled the raggedy ends of her days up
like bits of saved string,
tied her best bonnet beneath her chin,
and set off toward a green meadow
that no one sees but her.

She's done with it—
this life that's like a hound dog
whining at the back porch,
willing to settle for scraps.
She has no patience with a world
half-visible and barely heard.
Her dignity draped over her shoulders
like a shawl of fine old lace,
she aims her chin at the sun and walks,
done with relationships and sorrow.
Proud and submissive,
longing for rest,
undone and undaunted,
she will not be seen in this old world again.
She has gone to the valley.
She has taken the long walk.
She has traded her quilt-scraps for stars.

Albert Huffstickler

One Man's Family

in memory of Bill Gilmore

There was the Dog Man again today,
bent under his tow sack,
making his daily pilgrimage
along St. Mary's Street
with his rag tied to his forehead,
with his saintly leanness
and his bunch of seven dogs

and his clothes covered with
short smelly hair.
Pauline, the waitress up at
the White House Cafe, says
he used to be a college professor.
In a college. Imagine.
And now he's all the time
with them dogs.
Lets them sleep in the same room
with him. Lets them eat
the same thing he eats.
Pauline don't like it.
All them eyes that light up in the dark
like wolves'.

I imagine he carries his mother's
wedding dress around in that filthy sack.
I imagine he takes the dress out on Sundays
and talks to it about the dogs,
the way he might talk to Pauline
if she ever gave him the chance.
About how to him those seven dogs
are seven faithful wives,
seven loaves, seven brothers.

About how those seven snouts bulldozing
through neighborhood garbage and memories
give off a warmth that's just as good
as all the breasts and apple pies and Christmas trees
and books and pipes and slippers
that a man could use on this earth.

But mostly about how they're dogs.
Friends that don't have to be anything else.
About how nothing could be more right
than for a man to live
with what he is willing and able to trust.

Rosemary Catacalos

 W. S. Merwin   Andrea Carlisle

The Unwritten

Inside this pencil
crouch words that have never been written
never been spoken
never been taught

they're hiding

they're awake in there
dark in the dark
hearing us
but they won't come out
not for love not for time not for fire

even when the dark has worn away
they'll still be there
hiding in the air
multitudes in days to come may walk through them
breathe them
be none the wiser

what script can it be
that they won't unroll
in what language
would I recognize it
would I be able to follow it
to make out the real names
of everything

maybe there aren't
many
it could be that there's only one word
and it's all we need
it's here in this pencil
every pencil in the world
is like this

W. S. Merwin

Emily Dickinson's To-Do List
Sum-Sum-Summertime

Monday
Figure out what to wear—white dress?

Put hair in bun
Bake gingerbread for Sue
Peer out window at passersby
Write poem
Hide poem

Tuesday
White dress? Off-white dress?
Feed cats
Chat with Lavinia
Work in garden
Letter to T. W. H.

Wednesday
White dress or what?
Eavesdrop on visitors from behind door
Write poem
Hide poem

Thursday
Try on new white dress
Gardening—watch out for narrow fellows in grass!
Gingerbread, cakes, treats
Poems: Write and hide them

Friday
Embroider sash for white dress
Write poetry
Water flowers on windowsill
Hide everything

Andrea Carlisle

Sharif Elmusa   *Natasha Waxman*

A Little Piece of Sky

Marveling today at the Safeway's abundance
of tuna fish cans,
I thought of my friend Hussein.
He was the genius of the school.
He breathed in history, grammar, math
as easily as the dust of the camp.
He had a pyramid's core. Books
would've sprouted from his head,
but he had to live, and to live he
apprenticed with a carpenter,
and later on flew his skill to an oil country
where he made good as a contractor.

His father had been killed the spring he was born
in a familiar war that made us refugees
and tossed us on the moral map of the world.
His mother was a woman of meager means,
could look at a word for a year
and not recognize what it was.
And so it was:
poverty wagged him every day.

One afternoon
I met him walking from the store
holding, with his thumb and forefinger,

the upright lid of a half-opened
tuna fish can, humming a tune
about holding a little piece of sky.

Sharif Elmusa

War Rug

Step carefully please
there's a grenade nesting
in the pile of my carpet
the yellow one there
with the red border

Shape of interlocked flowers
identify the village of its provenance
but not the baby fingers
that knotted in
    the Kalashnikov rifle
    the Russian helicopter

The obscure geometry of war
is sketched in wool upon my floor—
But yellow is impartial,
the color of the mean, they say—

What god would I die for?
For what would I whirl in wind
a cardboard hanged-woman
beneath a bridge?

For what dye,
what tint to resist
the oppression of my ease?

Can the thread
be bitten through
as wool between the teeth
of a weaver?

Upstanding wool
that knelt on a lamb's back
was drenched in berry juice
and pollen pastes, left
to dry under the quenchless
Afghan sun, woven into its second day
by the small fingers of a watchful child,
bartered for my good clean dollars
for guns.

Oh child, are you the owl
perched unblinking
on the edge of the tank?

Or are you the funnel of black wool
interrupting the pattern,
headed for the rug's border?

Natasha Waxman

 Edward Field   Judith Steinbergh

Plant Poem

The shrimp plant on my desk had one long low branch
that moved mysteriously about,
turning to the sunlight outside
or, on dark days, toward the electric light inside.
You could actually see it travel with a kind of trembling.
Even when the sun was out
it might move across the table
and look right up at me where I sat.
It was like having a little friend, a pet.

I thought maybe the vibration of my typing
gave it the energy to do that.
Sometimes it moved and sometimes not,
it didn't always have the strength,
but the leaves could always swivel toward the light.
Finally it grew so long it got in my way
and in a merciless moment
I tied it upright to a stake.

I never again felt it looking at me.
I wonder if it was struggling to get free.

Edward Field

Letting the Parakeet Fly

In those hours I'm home among the still things,
paintings, plants, piles of clean laundry, drafts
of unfinished poems, I let the parakeet out of
his cage, free in the house, if one considers
that free. I do it, I think, to relieve the guilt
that comes from owning a caged bird in the first
place. Also I like the pale blue blurs it makes
crossing the room, crepe paper streamers or silk.
When it flaps its short take-offs and shorter
landings, a wind fills the room, a sound like
torches or locusts. While I work, I know that
among the quiet, something moves, breathes, makes
heat, weather, whole flocks of geese. Something
becomes more than it is, stirs up the mind,
the air. Sets my own words free.

Judith Steinbergh

 Robert Burlingame   *Linda Pastan*

small poems

the small poems
that speak of the breakage of time
are mysterious in them-
selves

they draw close
to the fresh mouths of children
they speak as little as they know how
patiently waiting

never telling how they got
here
they nevertheless shine
in their smallness, like murmured songs

in their lostness
they drift down like the floating
seeds of dandelions
tenacious, hopeful

so they catch in the high grass
or in the purely private
crevice of a city
gutter

      they're like snowflakes
new yellow leaves
or the wind-divided notes of meadowlarks
they drift bravely
to lodge in some forsaken place

there they change
they rot, melt, or sing
because it is all they can do
they are like everything

Robert Burlingame

Elegy

Somewhere a poem
is waiting for me
to write it: in the jewelry box,
coiled into an old ring
or stopping the hands
of a watch;
in the vanishing barn, risen
to the top of the pail
to be skimmed off;
or in the tree outside
engraved in green ink
on the underside of a leaf.

In my old room
the white curtains blow
like ghosts of themselves
over the sill;
under the bed misplaced words gather
to grab my helpless ankle.
It is a poem
the child I was hides
in the ear of the woman
I have become: a poem
whose lines were the lines
of my father's face.

Linda Pastan

Separate Longings

Roger Jones   *Yaedi Ignatow*

Revelations, First Time

So finally I came to it the spring
of my fifteenth year, that book
of the blood-red moon, spilt stars,
heavens gashed wide and glowing like
molten brass, the day at last arrived
for the world to drown in fire.

Outside, on tips of March limbs,
sweet-gum buds peered out meek as lambs;
pools from last week's showers glimmered,
pollen-lined as if with wobbly haloes.
On the phone line, a dove sat preaching
nothing like damnation or eternal ruin,

while indoors I met the wrath and power,
saw the end burst from cracked pages,
heard seals broken, felt the ground tremble
as all stood one by one to confess their deeds,
empires lying toppled and smoldering,
the voice of one above them clear as a cannon.

Shaken, I marked my place halfway and ran
to the garden to steady out my mind.
Behind the hedgerows, a quiet sun slipped down;

dogwood blooms hovered in wet gray stillness.
I gazed at my hands and arms, the temple of flesh:
mercy. Mercy was written everywhere.

Roger Jones

Androgeny

Androgeny is the universe
telling us where it began—
all energy packed into one
loving itself until it could stand it no more—
exploding into separate longings.

Yaedi Ignatow

 Arthur Sze   Marilyn Williams

The Shapes of Leaves

Ginkgo, cottonwood, pin oak, sweet gum, tulip tree:
our emotions resemble leaves and alive
to their shapes we are nourished.

Have you felt the expanse and contours of grief
along the edges of a big Norway maple?
Have you winced at the orange flare

searing the curves of a curling dogwood?
I have seen from the air logged islands,
each with a network of branching gravel roads,

and felt a moment of pure anger, aspen gold.
I have seen sandhill cranes moving in an open field,
a single white whooping crane in the flock.

And I have traveled along the contours
of leaves that have no name. Here
where the air is wet and the light is cool,

I feel what others are thinking and do not speak,
I know pleasure in the veins of a sugar maple,
I am living at the edge of a new leaf.

Arthur Sze

Images

Through an angled mirror
I saw my selves receding
One by one—leaves falling
Downward from a tree.
Alone, I turned to go.
They turned to disappear
Farther into the mirror.
This was long ago.

Now it is very strange.
They are coming back to join me
Out of the mirror.
I am more startled than a tree
When leaves appear.

Marilyn Williams

 Richard Peabody   Ellen Bryant Voigt

Burning the Dolls

Not really hate, or some demento girl-boy thing.
Just curiosity and being around them day-in, day-out,
scattered across my sister's lily-white dresser.
And having moved on naturally from zapping
ants with a magnifying glass, to disfiguring
toy soldiers with a woodburning kit, and still further
to torching model airplanes, the dolls were simply
the next logical step, since we couldn't buy flamethrowers.

We dragged Barbie, Ken, Skipper and Midge, along
with Chatty Cathy and anybody else we could find
out into the backyard, stripped them down, positioned
them provocatively astride each other, doused them
with lighter fluid and had a plastic bonfire.
The results kind of reminded me of a Vincent Price
film—*House of Wax*. Torsos melting one way,
limbs another, heads imploding like smashed pumpkins.

The smoke was black, green and gray. Perfect
preparation for what would happen during wartime.

Richard Peabody

The Field Trip

This time they're thirteen, no longer
interested in the trillium on the path but in each other,
though they will not say so. Only the chaperone
lingers at the adder's tongue,
watching the teacher trail the rest uphill
to where the dense virginal forest thins and opens.
At the clearing, she tells them to be still and mute
and make a list of what they see and hear.
A girl asks if she should also list
the way she feels—she's the one
who'll cite the shadow on the lake below.
The others sprawl on gender-separate rocks
except for the smart-ass, perched
on the cliff edge, inviting front-page photos—
PICNIC MARRED BY TRAGEDY. From time to time,
in the midst of the day's continual lunch,
as the students read the lists their teacher edits,
the boy swears and stretches—
he is in fact fourteen, doing seventh grade
a second time, this same assignment
also a second time. Pressed, he says
he sees exactly what he saw before—ponds, rocks, trees—

shouting it back from the same vantage point
out on the twelve-inch ledge,
Long Pond a ragged puddle underneath him;
and what he shouts grows more and more
dangerously insubordinate as he leans
more and more dramatically over the edge.
But he is, after all, the first to spot the hawk;
and it is, looking down on it, amazing. The others
gather near the unimpeded view,
together, finally, standing on this bluff
overlooking three natural ponds, hearing the wind
ruffle the cedar fringe, watching the hawk
float along the thermals like a leaf.
And for a moment, belittled by indifferent wilderness,
you want to praise the boy, so much does he resemble
if not the hawk then the doomed shrub
fanned against the rockface there beside him,
rooted in a fissure in the rock.
But soon the hero swings back up to earth,
the group divides. Just like that
they're ready for home, tired of practicing:
sixteen children, two adults and one
bad boy who carved a scorpion on his arm.

Ellen Bryant Voigt

Charles Simic

Andrea Potos

Summer Morning

I love to stretch
Like this, naked
On my bed in the morning;
Quiet, listening:

Outside they are opening
Their primers
In the little school
Of the cornfield.

There is a smell of damp hay,
Of horses, of summer sky,
Of laziness, of eternal life.

I know all the dark places
Where the sun hasn't reached yet,
Where the singing has just ceased
In the hidden aviaries of the crickets—
Anthills where it goes on raining—
Slumbering spiders dreaming of wedding dresses.

I pass over the farmhouses
Where the little mouths open to suck,
Barnyards where a man, naked to the waist,
Washes his face with a hose,
Where the dishes begin to rattle in the kitchen.

The good tree with its voice
Of a mountain brook
Knows my steps
It hushes.

I stop and listen:
Somewhere close by
A stone cracks a knuckle,
Another turns over in its sleep.

I hear a butterfly stirring
In the tiny soul of the caterpillar.
I hear the dust dreaming
Of eyes and great winds.

Further ahead, someone
Even more silent
Passes over the grass
Without bending it.

—And all of a sudden
In the midst of that silence
It seems possible
To live simply
On the earth.

Charles Simic

Depending on the Light

I roll the red cake of lipstick
slowly over my lips and lean closer to the mirror,
        seeing my mother again
coloring carefully inside the lines,
while I'd sit on the edge of her bed
when she started from scratch
to *put on her face*
before my father got home—
pink rouge spiralled over her cheekbones,
the excess dabbed off with a small, round sponge;
eyeshadow flecked with silver
glinting like mica from a blue stream;
the long tube of mascara she used—
her lashes molded stiff
and sticky as tar; then the measured press of her lips together
making sure they were evenly red. And lastly her arms—
    arced like a dancer
around her head, a can of Aqua Net in her right hand
while she sprayed into dark sculpture her hair
that turned a shining auburn
depending on the light,
just as so much depended
on the shading in his voice,
his glance when he'd return home late—his eyes
painting their approval on her.

Andrea Potos

Shuntarō Tanikawa *Diane Hina Kahanu*

August

August is a dreamless month
I saw
everywhere the blue sea
and thighs of sun-tanned girls
I saw!
The sun shifting
the wind sweeping the shore
and then
my blood and the sea and the night
all took on the same smell.
Other than that there was nothing
other than that
there was
nothing
August
was filled with the glory of this star.

Shuntarō Tanikawa
Translated by Harold Wright

When I Was Young on an Island

When I was young on an island
my brother caught gray baby sharks
on his bamboo fishing pole.

When he'd catch a shark,
he'd call the other kids and
we'd come running with clubs
of driftwood to beat the shark
to death.

When I was young on an island
my brother made moray eel traps
of silver pineapple juice cans
and a can opener, the kind that
makes triangle holes. When he'd
catch an eel, he'd give it to the
neighbor cat and we'd all watch
the tiger-striped cat
take the eel out of the can
and eat it.

When we were young on Paikō Drive
in Kuli'ou'ou and we played war,
my brother invented the battle charge.
He'd wait for a hard wind to pick
up the sand and just when the wind
was strongest, he'd yell, "Charge,"
and we'd run, head down, into a zillion
tiny bullets of stinging sand
hurled by the wind's hand.

When we were young on an island
my brother invented the jellyfish
test. He was an Apache Indian that day.
Tortured, he would not cry out.

We caught see-through jellyfish
in our hands and held them
while they stung us. Whoever
cried out first or dropped their
jellyfish lost. I remember sinking
to my knees with pain and finally
laying down in the cool, shallow water.
Only my burning jellyfish hand
held out.

Diane Hina Kahanu

 Paul B. Janeczko   *Lucille Clifton*

How to Hug
Your Three-Year-Old Daughter

(for Emma)

Be prepared
to be quick.

The hug may come
when you expect it least:
you're carrying a cup of hot coffee
    answering her call sleepy eyed
        lifting bread from the oven.

The hug may come
around your knees
before she darts off
or from behind
as you stoop
to fish the remote
from beneath the couch.

Don't be afraid
to ask for one.
Get down on your knees.
Spread your arms
to improve her aim.
Close your eyes.
Let her eager abruptness
startle you.
Grin.
Remember:
tomorrow is prompt.

Be prepared
to be quick.

Paul B. Janeczko

4 daughters

i am the sieve she strains from
little by little
everyday.

i am the rind
she is discarding.

i am the riddle
she is trying to answer.

something is moving
in the water.
she is the hook.
i am the line.

Lucille Clifton

 David Clewell   Alise Alousi

Disappearing

People always find you.

They'll find the napkin
you shredded in a diner in New Jersey.
The red light you drove through
a few miles north of there.

The tree you leaned against
at 3 in the morning.

These people are unscrupulous;
they'll make the pieces fit.

You cannot even trust the night.
Someone walking in the opposite direction
will recognize your face with its tired grin.
He'll pin you down in your new neighborhood
like a butterfly in the wrong country.

To disappear
you must move among them at noon.
Be gentle with their daughters.
Wear shoes that leave discernible tracks.

Learn to speak a few words well,
and they may believe you
when you tell them
you have been here all along.

David Clewell

Medusa Cement

She took
what i said
and put it
in her hair
her hair which
spiraled to
the floor or
on occasion
floated to
the ceiling.

She took
what i said
and ground it
up really small
it was some words
she put them
into the building
i mean when
the building
was built
facing the water
on that side
my words were
mixed in.

Alise Alousi

Paul Durcan   *Paulette Jiles*

The Lion Tamer

"Well, what do you work at?" she said to me after about six
    months
Of what a mutual journalist friend was pleased to call our
    "relationship."
"I'm a lion tamer," I replied, offhandedly as possible,
Hoping she'd say: "Are you really?"
Instead she said: "I don't believe you."
I jumped up from my chair and I strode across the room,
Stumbling over a wickerwork magazine rack.
I knelt on one knee at her feet and gazed up at her:
Slowly she edged away from me and backed out the door
And glancing out the window I saw her bounding down the
    road,
Her fair hair gleaming in the wind, her crimson voice growling.
I kicked over a stool and threw my whip on the floor.
What I had hoped for from her was a thorough mauling.
But she preferred artistic types. She had no appetite for lion
    tamers.

Paul Durcan

Tallness

This man is much taller than I am;
his feet hang out but mine
are still covered
in the middle of the night.

Mostly I look at his shirt pocket;
he can only see
the top of my head.

I can feel his gaze dripping
over my crown like a broken
egg, slithering down.

Everyone is afraid of broken yolks like that,
howler monkeys, guinea hens.

Who knows what men are thinking,
what eggs they are
sticking their long-nailed thumbs into?

Paulette Jiles

Gregory Orr   *Daisy Zamora*

Who'd Want to Be a Man?

With his heart
a black sack
in which a small
animal's trapped.

With his grief
like a knot
that's tied at birth,
balled up and hard.

With his rage
that would smash
the ten thousand things
without blinking.

With his mind
like a tree on a cliff—
its roots, fists
clutching stone.

With his longing
that's a dry well
and where is the rain?

Gregory Orr

To Be a Woman

Having been born a woman
means placing your body at the service of others
giving your time to others
thinking only in terms of others.

Having been born a woman
means that your body is not yours
your time is not yours
your thoughts do not belong to you.

Being born a woman
is being born into nothingness.
If it weren't that your body-home
insures the continuance of the species
you might as well not have been born.

To be born a woman
is to come to nothing,
to a life you do not inhabit
in which everyone else—not your own heart—
determines and decides.

To be born a woman
is to be at the bottom of the well, the moat,
the pit that surrounds the walled city
where They live, They alone: those
you are called to admire, trick, charm,
humiliating and selling yourself.
You must swim against all currents,

rebel, fight, and scream
until you can push the boulders apart
and slip out through the crack,
destroying the draw bridge, tearing down the walls,
making it to the moat and crossing the chasm,
leaping without wings from the precipice
impelled only by your heart
sustained only by your mind
until you have liberated yourself
from the nothingness you will only conquer
with your woman's voice, your verb.

Daisy Zamora
Translated by Margaret Randall and Elinor Randall

 David Ignatow   Leslie Ullman

Lunchtime

None said anything startling from the rest;
each held her coffee cup in her own way,
and one twanged, another whined and a third
shot out her phrases like a rear exhaust
yet each stood for the same things:
the clothes in their conversation,
the food they ate and the men they could not
catch up with. They were not saying more
than could be said in a crowd, they made this
their unity, as the thinking of one person;

and getting up to go, lunch over
by the clock, each pulled out her own chair
from underneath her.

David Ignatow

Peace

Keep your voice down, my husband
hissed this morning across his plate,
then knotted his tie
to a fist that would hold
all day. Wedged in our thin
walls against the silence of neighbors
we haven't met, I folded
my napkin, shoved the last word
back in my throat
and later jogged extra laps
as though my feet could make
some mark on firm ground,
could make everything clear.
I remove my damp
sweatclothes, shivering now
in the best boutique I can find.
An older woman shrugs out of a fur
soft as fog and gathers up jade, silver,
apple-green silks, all hushed
and viciously expensive.

She wraps herself in a gown
the color of doves, a shadow body
that follows no husband. I'm sure their house
holds a room where she dreams,
sends letters, while someone downstairs
seasons the greens and filets
and a reasonable hunger warms her like firelight.
If her children should quarrel
on the darkening lawn she drifts outside
to soothe each with a story, her voice adding
girth to itself like the wine,
open, breathing by his plate.

I want to ask for my size
in a gown like hers. I want to fill
a gown with breasts like hers, and move
through our rooms like a boat
through any water. I finger aqua silk
made for real hips and shoulders
I, too, could have after twenty seasons—

it turns a whole room blue
where I enter myself as I dress,
where my garments turn overhead light
back on itself like fine paintings.
Downstairs he slices meat striped with fat
and pink flesh, while I finger each
pearl on the choker he gave me when money
was tight. The blue folds drift
over my body, that house
filled with rooms left by daughters

and sons, that house given over
to pale silk and stone, its silence
my secret, my eyes raised
to meet hers in the triple mirror.

Leslie Ullman

Ted Kooser   Jeannette Doob

The Onion Woman

All of the clothes she owns
she wears in layers, coat
upon coat upon coat
like an onion. She's wrapped
the woman inside, the taste
of the woman, her odors,
her heart. But the fear
still shows through all those skins—
that tight white core
where the shoot has withered.

Ted Kooser

My Mother's Blue Vase

She never brought flowers
into the house.
They were full of insects,
ants that would march
along the table and disturb
the sugar bowl.

Stacks of *True Story* magazines
lay near the treadle sewing
machine in the basement.
On the shelf above was
the deep blue vase
I'd rolled a marble into,
its white swirling surface
lodged in the neck, a half-moon
shining in the darkness.

Now that there are spots
on my hands and pale green
spiders in the curve of roses
on my table, I wonder

When did she decide it was
too much trouble to dream?

Jeannette Doob

Shuntarō Tanikawa   Margo LaGattuta

Everyone

Everyone possesses something sad
and hides it in silence from everyone.
ha ha ha
Everyone possesses something unforgivable
keeping it possessed without forgiveness.
ha ha ha
At night   before going to bed
everyone has one look of sadness
like a rabbit or a snake
a look that sees nothing at all.
ha ha ha
Everyone possesses something unspeakable
so without knowing what to say
he possesses it all alone.
ha ha ha ha ha ha ha ha ha
So sometimes suddenly
    he wants to do something
        like kiss a girl
forcing her tongue down with his own
firmly for a long time
and then ruthlessly open his eyes
to look at the distant sky
    or in the direction of the hills.

Shuntarō Tanikawa
Translated by Harold Wright

String Affair

One string is waiting
to be looped by another.
It is trying the impossible trick
of hanging free around a box
of Chinese wind socks,
pretending not to want
closure, or anything that
seductive. Just a frayed
end flapping in the breeze.
Just a white moment
pausing to reflect upon
its own significant other
string, which is nowhere
to be found in this
package. Not to be
undone or tied up
is the string's peace now.
Not to be seen wanting
gives a certain twist on grief.

Margo LaGattuta

 William Freedman   Marilyn Nelson

The Family

Annie Green,
mother of Roosevelt,
twenty-eight, of Georgia,
convicted of the kidnap,
rape, and murder
of a girl, eighteen,
watched his execution
by electric chair.
The papers said she
kept her calm.
A little tight about the lips,
but calm,
the boy a little tight
about the thighs
when they strapped him in,
but calm.
God was with him
in his innocence, he said.
He hoped He was with others,
he had been reborn.
His father,
though he wished to be there,
had to wait outside.
They were afraid
he would not keep calm.
When it was over

the doctor,
a little pale but calm,
emerged to tell him
mother and son were doing fine.

William Freedman

April
Rape

Bessie Altmann is home again,
locked in so tight she can't take a breath,
the mouths of all the locks in the house
snatch at her air like cats.

But she wants it this way.
She likes the house tight as a skin
corset around her waist,
no breeze to wrap fingers there
and whisper like he did
please please please.

Bessie Altmann avoids mirrors,
dark eyes that look into hers:
Let me go.

It is April in Philadelphia,
in her two rooms she breathes
and breathes again her body's smell.
She wants to hide in a book,

small enough to slip unnoticed
between the lines of black print
and never be seen again.

She considers alternatives:
A knife. A razor blade tucked
neatly between lip and gum.
Karate. Mace. A gun.
But she knows these will never work.

She is trying to grow teeth everywhere.
She will bite the next man that comes,
eat him up like a piece of ice.
She is glad to be home again.

Marilyn Nelson

 Wing Tek Lum   *Jane Mayhall*

On M. Butterfly

The man who waits at the bus stop every night for his wife
    as an act of love
The man who bakes pastries the way they do in Hong Kong
    without much sugar
The man who drives a taxi with photos of his daughters
    propped on his dashboard
sees in movies
    the detective with his eyes made up
walking about on dainty feet

The man whose bookkeeping makes him a hero
    at the nursing home
The man who moonlights as a full time cook
    after his day at the supermarket
The man who applies lacquer with a Chinese brush
    to the furniture he has made
watches on television
    the faceless gangsters in pin stripe suits
lugging briefcases with opium and laundered money

The man who swears his daily tai chi exercise
    helps him sell insurance
The man who gave up golf for narcissus bulbs
    and has never regretted it
The man who always argues with his father at their store
    and then drives with him back home
follows on the stage
    a pale spy in flowing robes
dressed like a woman to deceive men

Wing Tek Lum

Tracing Back

My mother took care of my father's shirts;
he did not take care of her cotton dresses.
I think he would have been ashamed,
not of the labor, but of a peculiar
sense of squalor, a man wasting his time,

winding his arms around the soiled garments,
the daily plethora, and humble sheddings.
What grim, unpresiding angel, drooped and dull?
Both of them, a part of the aboriginal pool.

Jane Mayhall

 James Tate   *Donna Trussell*

A Missed Opportunity

A word sits on the kitchen counter
next to the pitcher of cream
with its blue cornflowers bent.
Perhaps a guest left it in a hurry
or as a tip for good service,
or as a fist against some imagined
insult. Or it fell with some old
plaster from the ceiling, a word
some antediluvian helpmate
hushed up. It picked itself up
from the floor, brushed itself off
and, somehow, scratched its way
up the cupboards. It appears to be
a word of considerable strength
and even significance, but I can't
bring myself to look into its gaze.
The cornflowers are pointing toward
the cookies not far away. An expert

could be called to defuse the word,
but it is Sunday and they are still
sleeping or singing, and, besides that,
the word seems to have moved again
on its own, and now it appears warm
and welcoming, it throbs with life
and a sincere desire to understand me.
It looks slightly puzzled and hurt,
as though I . . . I take a step toward it,
I hold out my hand. "Friend," I say,
but it is shrinking, it is going away
to its old home in the familiar
cold dark of the human parking lot.

James Tate

Snow

She packs her suitcase—
mad red socks
and tough denim.

He does not touch her shoulders.
He folds his arms,
leans against the wall.

says, I don't know why,
people change.
He walks away.

She returns her suitcase
to the spiders
and dust.

Night brings broken sleep
and cliffs dissolving
under her shoes.

She combs her hair.
Her hands
are rubber gloves.

The next four days she eats
nothing.
Help me, she whispers.

His face is shut.
She's seen this face before.
It's the face he turned

to the old man downstairs
whose car was stuck
in the snow.

Donna Trussell

Reginald Gibbons   *Thylias Moss*

We Say

We say a heart breaks—like
a stick, maybe, or a bottle
or a wave. But it seems, too,
like the consuming flame
of a moment, the field clump
that crackles upward from a match
and collapses, grass filaments
glowing in the ash-dust
then going out. Today
I take myself down by steps,
one at a time, into the sadness
I admit I can't always reach.
There should be a room
at the bottom of the black stairway,
my friends sitting with strangers,
waiting, but there's no one,
only the memory, when
the pale air flickers as if
it were an invisible flame,
of my aunt in her hospital bed
and beside her, about to be left
alone—the last sister, and so soon—
my mother, bent over
the purse in her lap, eyes closed.
I can see the patent leather gloss
and the shiny clasp that until

just now she had been
snapping open and shut, till—
just now—it broke. That breaking—
like a voice that cracks, cursing
or crying, or the song that falls,
out of thinking too far ahead,
into a smoldering loneliness—
was that the sound of the heart?

Reginald Gibbons

Dennis's Sky Leopard

He saw it first, me just the big, the
little dippers and questions about
when they'd be full, ready to pour
something into me, anything, not just
what I've needed so long I've forgotten
what it is. He said

"I love him." How familiar
that sounded; I love him too, the one
steering the planets, a very male
thing to do; a woman admits to difficulty
in just navigating one small life, maneuvering
it away from diapers, last minute trips to Messina's
for bell peppers that don't chime, for both
angel and devil's food cake mixes to hide the truth,
for sugarless gum, sugarless colas and lemon limes,
ginger drinks full of pin pricks,

because the honeymoon is over; the grace period
is gone; the music must be faced now, rock lyrics
that slap with the full force of Rolling Stones,
verifying that you're the only sinner in the world.
Dennis said, "He's up in the air." I tried
to suck him up my nose. Dennis said, "He can't
come down." So he defies gravity, he breaks
bad laws, he's a male Antigone, a man I'd like
to meet if he weren't a leopard
and without domestic instincts like men.

This leopard takes up the whole sky, decorated
(as in purple, love-bruised hearts)
with constellations, star-quality spots.
He lives better up there than in the jungle.
Rain is attempt at spot give-away. They melt.
Something about our atmosphere and hospitality.

I tilt my head, let it rain in my throat. Inside
I feel like a wheat field ready for perfect
harvest leading to ultimate feast but I'm never
cut down. That's the best part.

Thylias Moss

 Ronald Wallace   Linda Pastan

Wild Strawberries

In this weedy field somewhere inside marriage,
snuggled under thistles and nettles, we find them,
bright promises. Down on our knees like penitents
or children, we pick, our tongues puckered and bloodied,
our careless hands stung red, the sun plumping
ripe and peppery in the July sky.

This morning we fought over nothing
I can remember, pride springing up all around us,
with its barbs and hooks. Now all afternoon
I've been thinking how we'll grow old together,
our perennial violence and tenderness,
bearing less and less.

Back in the city, the markets stock strawberries
bred for safe shipment, long storage,
crisp and predictable in their stacked flats.
Here, as we carry our berries back to the cabin,
back to our dangerous lives,
we know they are so fragile and ripe

their own weight in the bowl could ruin or bruise them
beyond texture, or beauty, or definition.

Ronald Wallace

Camellias

I drag the lawn chair
to the center of the new lawn
where you have warned
it will ruin the delicate
grass. From here
I have a perfect view
of the pink camellia,
the one with rose-shaped flowers
which you secretly think
I have ignored. This is my camellia
viewing platform
I tell you, remembering
signposts in Japan.

You look at the dark cave
beneath my chair where the grass
will die in architectural stripes.
We look at each other.
This is one of the impasses
a marriage must
make a detour around
or else crash into.
Meanwhile the camellia
opens its flesh-colored petals
with utter unself-consciousness,
releasing its scent
into the dangerous air.

Linda Pastan

George Eklund — *Lois Marie Harrod*

Dressing My Daughter

I have solved the riddle
of the three white buttons
but now you twist away from me
and all the muscle of my heart
must hold
and help you understand—
Your mother has told me twice
the tiny pink bows
on these white anklets
must be turned
outward for the world
to see, to understand
you are a girl-child
and the pink bows
will help them see you
and help them remember
the words they are
to say.

George Eklund

Fitting Room

(for my daughter Katy)

My mother loved me in my green prom dress,
her favorite color, but I will love you in any shade,
in the third grade it was always purple,

and I am watching your white socks now
as in the fitting room next to you, a girl,
your age, is stepping into a red prom dress.

Her feet are sweaty and pink on the orange carpet,
wrinkled like yours when you sluff off your shoes,
and somebody's watching her, too, a brother maybe,

a boyfriend slouched in the chair beside me,
Guns N' Roses T-shirt, denim jacket,
picking his teeth, chewing his nails,

and as you appear in white linen, she opens
her door too, her eyes begging him
to love it, her hair defiant—

red is not her color, nor is blonde,
and he grunts up and shuffles toward her,
touches her bare shoulder with one hand and shrugs.

She shuts the door, taffeta whispering
to her hand, and he leans forward seeing more
than a red dress dropping at her feet,

while you are showing me your second choice,
pink and cotton, you are so much thinner than you were,
and I'll buy either, I'll buy both.

I am thinking how beautiful your hair is,
its own soft color, and when she shows him
the second dress, black, he stands, twirls her around,

his hands clumsy on her blemished back,
and then I want her to be as beautiful as you,
whom no one has told what to wear,
and no one has yet asked to dance.

Lois Marie Harrod

 Michael Burns   *Del Marie Rogers*

Beginnings

When we drive in the mist to town together
this morning, my four-year-old son
and I, he stays very quiet, and I don't know whether
he's thinking about something he's seen
out the fogged window, some other
time, or only of what he soon
must do: take his coat off, kiss me goodbye,
become himself alone for one more day.

He comes to me this evening after school
completely changed. No silence now,
he struts about the room, full
of the day and himself, but I still want to know
more than he plans to tell
about his work, friends, everything new.
OK, he says, we learned to hurt bad guys.
We had to fix the room back like it was.

On TV, after supper, it's loss again,
people blown out of each other's lives,
or it's drugs and money, a sad cop with a gun.
Easily amused, we've cuddled and laughed
in the big chair until we're tired. We've gone
already to get our drink, to loaf
before a window, and Mother and sister have said
good night. Daddy, he says, don't ever be dead.

Michael Burns

Late, Watching Television

I call up the handful of planets close enough
for contact, ask a bright face at the other end
of each light-beam, What do we have?
How long? Each body flickers, shimmers.
Screen faces are earnest, brief.

But I'm secure in deep home dark,
my face lit only with distant rose.

That light is the secret of watching. I ask
What are the links between us?
In a hundred years, who will know me?

They're full of gossip, the week's surprises.
They want to talk about something else.

Del Marie Rogers

 Kurtis Lamkin   *Martha Zweig*

Golden Season

I shoulder my son over dead stalks,
feel him up there rocking,
a captain taller than we'll ever be alone.

He trips cornrows like a one-man
kindergarten, scattering south
toward woods senile in the far haze.

If I could teach him I would tell him
men are longitude, women latitude
but wherever you stand is the top of the world.

What else can you tell a boy
who likes flying, sparrows, tumbling
and being amazed?

You know he's not a herd of palominos
but he thinks he's free.

Kurtis Lamkin

Dark Song

Don't be scared of the dark;
in your tidy room in the dark there is
no hard heart;
you fit into your bed in the dark
like a secret into an ear,
dark to repeat it, dark to overhear.

Don't be scared of the dark:
all night is is the biggest shadow,
little kid in the biggest shadow, it's
how you can tell the sun's behind the world
when the sun's gone,
when the sun's gone.

Day gone, daylight gone;
think about dark to all the things with no-eyes:
how dark cools off the meadow stones,
how dark stops the sugar work in the leaves,
how dark bends the tall grass
stalks over all wet. Don't scare

easy of any
such deep deep dark, how it is, the
toys, your favorites, turtle, cat,
stuffed and buttoned; and who
carries you keeps you, dark doesn't, no dark
doesn't, I do.

Martha Zweig

 Robert Bly   *Judith Hemschemeyer*

Driving My Parents Home at Christmas

As I drive my parents home through the snow,
their frailty hesitates on the edge of a mountainside.
I call over the cliff,
only snow answers.
They talk quietly
of hauling water, of eating an orange,
of a grandchild's photograph left behind last night.
When they open the door of their house, they disappear.
And the oak when it falls in the forest who hears it
    through miles and miles of silence?
They sit so close to each other . . . as if pressed together
        by the snow.

Robert Bly

I Remember the Room Was Filled with Light

They were still young, younger than I am now.
I remember the room was filled with light
And moving air. I was watching him
Pick brass slivers from his hands as he did each night
After work. Bits of brass gleamed on his brow.
She was making supper. I stood on the rim
Of a wound just healing; so when he looked up
And asked me when we were going to eat
I ran to her, though she could hear. She smiled
And said, "Tell him . . ." Then "Tell her . . . " On winged feet
I danced between them, forgiveness in my cup,
Wise messenger of the gods, their child.

Judith Hemschemeyer

 Philip Booth   *Jane Kenyon*

Was It

Was it he said she said or
what she said he said?
         What
I hate isn't your getting old,
it's your letting me get old.

Philip Booth

Coats

I saw him leaving the hospital
with a woman's coat over his arm.
Clearly she would not need it.
The sunglasses he wore could not
conceal his wet face, his bafflement.

As if in mockery the day was fair,
and the air mild for December. All the same
he had zipped his own coat and tied
the hood under his chin, preparing
for irremediable cold.

Jane Kenyon

 Gerald Stern   George Ella Lyon

Romance

After thirty years
I am still listening to the pipes,
I am still enchanted
with the singing and moaning of the dry boards.

I am lying there night after night
thinking of water.
I am joining palms, or whistling Mozart
and early Yeats.

I am living without savagery,
stretching my body and turning on my left side
for music,
humming to myself and turning on my right side
for words.

Gerald Stern

Archaeology

I am digging
with a soft brush   a pen
at the site of my founding city
                Mothers
                        Fathers

I am listening
where the dirt flakes
from the dish chip
for a song my great-great
a hundred greats grandmother sang
way up the chromosome chain
                Shularoon
                        Shularoon

And the mountain speaks through its clay flute
and feet dance up and down its back
brushing off the light of this page

to sift through dark rooms
dust of a house I never entered
by the window where I make my bread.

George Ella Lyon

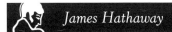

James Hathaway   *Marge Piercy*

The Congressman Visits the Grade School

In America we don't say things straight.
The Congressman has come today to praise

the children for their attendance & to present
the school with a flag that flew once

over our nation's capital. He tries to speak,
but a storm of raucous grackles,

gathered in the surrounding oaks,
eat his words. The Congressman pauses to mop

his brow. The children watch the bush
behind him dance with butterflies as large as

his handkerchief. They surge restlessly
in the heat, forward & back,

almost flood past the teachers, drown
the podium. When the talking is done,

the Congressman poses for pictures with
the future, his wide face beaming

among the lively young bodies. "Who knows, b-but
one day one of you may serve with me," he stutters.

While the camera focuses, little hands
shoot up like ferns, like tropical vines growing

all around the Congressman, one hand curling, unfurling
behind his head, fingers forming the primordial V.

James Hathaway

The Secretary Chant

My hips are a desk.
From my ears hang
chains of paper clips.
Rubber bands form my hair.
My breasts are wells of mimeograph ink.
My feet bear casters.
Buzz. Click.
My head
is a badly organized file.
My head is a switchboard
where crossed lines crackle.

My head is a wastebasket
of worn ideas.
Press my fingers
and in my ears appear
credit and debit.
Zing. Tinkle.
My naval is a reject button.
From my mouth issue canceled reams.
Swollen, heavy, rectangular
I am about to be delivered
of a baby
Xerox machine.
File me under W
because I wonce
was a woman.

Marge Piercy

 Tom Clark   Marilyn Nelson

Mountain Men

Names like Conger, Bridger, Rollins, Meeker, Berthoud
Echo through these canyons
Like summer thunder, proud and bold.
John Quincy Adams Rollins
Built the first wagon road through
The Great Divide. What didn't Sam Conger do?
A mile from here, you can call his name

And hear your voice return
Twelve times from the deepest shaft
Of the Conger mine. And you know Jim Bridger.

Men of ruthless ego all. But what of mountain ladies?
Didn't they too have pride? And what about
The narrowing ache in the bed beside
You when she wakes up to a rough face
That epitomizes 100 years of unpleasant history?

Tom Clark

Bali Hai Calls Mama

As I was putting away the groceries
I'd spent the morning buying
for the week's meals I'd planned
around things the baby could eat,
things my husband would eat,
and things I should eat
because they aren't too fattening,
late on a Saturday afternoon
after flinging my coat on a chair
and wiping the baby's nose
while asking my husband
what he'd fed it for lunch
and whether
the medicine I'd brought for him
had made his cough improve,
wiping the baby's nose again,

checking its diaper,
stepping over the baby
who was reeling to and from
the bottom kitchen drawer
with pots, pans, and plastic cups,
occasionally clutching the hem of my skirt
and whining to be held,
I was half listening for the phone
which never rings for me
to ring for me
and someone's voice to say that
I could forget about handing back
my students' exams which I'd had for a week,
that I was right about *The Waste Land*,
that I'd been given a raise,
all the time wondering
how my sister was doing,
whatever happened to my old lover(s),
and why my husband wanted
a certain brand of toilet paper,
and I wished I hadn't, but I'd bought
another fashion magazine that promised
to make me beautiful by Christmas,
and there wasn't room for the creamed corn
and every time I opened the refrigerator door
the baby rushed to grab whatever was on the bottom shelf
which meant I constantly had to wrestle
jars of its mushy food out of its sticky hands
and I stepped on the baby's hand and the baby was screaming
and I dropped the bag of cake flour I'd bought to make cookies
    with

and my husband rushed in to find out what was wrong because
    the baby
was drowning out the sound of the touchdown although I had
    scooped
it up and was holding it in my arms so its crying was inside
my head like an echo in a barrel and I was running cold water
on its hand while somewhere in the back of my mind wondering
    what
to say about *The Waste Land* and whether I could get away with
    putting
broccoli in a meatloaf when

suddenly through the window
came the wild cry of geese.

Marilyn Nelson

 Li-Young Lee   Linda Hogan

Here I Am

I wait. I don't go. He will come, the one
who waited for me each day
at the edge of the schoolyard.

I wait. And I am bitten thin
by waiting. And I grow
dense with luggage and time.

He will come, though
he may never come, who wrote his name
by drawing a spear borne in a heart.

In this life, this is how
one must wait, past despair,
the heart a fossil, the minutes molten, the feet turned to stone.

I know a boy who fell asleep
one second before his father returned, his name
a lozenge thinning on his father's tongue.

I've heard of prisoners who died
a minute before rescue.
Such waiting has nothing to do with hope;

it has less to do with patience;
it's simply the way a soul is bent.
Such waiting is impossible.

But I wait,
for it's the only
possibility left to me.

And though I stopped waiting years ago,
I continue to wait.
Even now

he comes, whom death has made giant.
And small as the rain
and as many.

Whose Sabbath shoes
I blackened each Saturday
and buffed to hard armor.

Who set me on a chair and two dictionaries
and made me read an old book
of ancient and terrifying stories

while sucking butterscotch drops
he unwrapped for me.
Sweet learning, he called it.

Even now,
no one comes,
though I sense his pure approach.

Maybe he is lost,
the lonely one
who is no longer lonely.

Maybe he waits for me.
Maybe he fears he is forgotten,
the way I am forgotten,

each of us the one
who, in that childhood game, shouts,
though no one hears, *Here I am!*

Li-Young Lee

The Lost Girls

I don't remember when
the girl of myself turned her back
and walked away, that girl
whose thin arms
once held this body
and refused to work too hard
or listen in school,
said the hell then
and turned,
that dark child,
that laugher and weeper
without shame, who turned
and skipped away.

And that other one
gone from me
and me
not even starting to knot
in vein or joint,
that curving girl
I loved to love with,
who danced away
the leather of red high heels
and thin legs, dancing like stopping
would mean the end of the world
and it does.

We go on
or we don't,
knowing about our inner women
and when they left us
like we were bad mothers or lovers
who wronged ourselves.

Some days it seems
one of them is watching, a shadow
at the edge of woods
with loose hair
clear down the back
and arms with dark moles
crossed before the dress I made
with my two red hands.

You there, girl, take my calloused hand.
I'm going to laugh and weep tonight,
quit all my jobs and I mean it this time,
do you believe me? I'm going to
put on those dancing shoes
and move till I can't stand
it anymore,
then touch myself clear down
to the sole of each sweet foot. That's all
the words I need,
not poems, not that talking mother
I was with milk and stories
peeking in at night,
but that lover of the moon
dancing outside when no one looks,

all right, then, even when they do,
and kissing each leaf of trees and squash,
and loving all the girls and women
I have always been.

Linda Hogan

Travelling Together

If we are separated I will
try to wait for you
on your side of things

your side of the wall and the water
and of the light moving at its own speed
even on leaves that we have seen
I will wait on one side

while a side is there

W. S. Merwin

Contributors' Notes

The contributors to this volume were sent a list of questions that asked them to consider the role gender has played in their lives and in their work. The following notes reflect their answers to those questions.

Francisco X. Alarcón (California) / According to the Nahuatl mythology, the universe began when Ometecuhtli and Omecihuatl (Lord and Lady of Duality) made love—this corresponds to the Western Big Bang theory of how the universe started. Men and women are equal and sacred, like the air they breathe, the water they drink, all the food they take from Mother Earth, including the humble tomatoes that are blessings to any kitchen.

Pam Alexander (Massachusetts) / Only after I was an adult did I see how important gender roles had been when I was growing up. I was allowed to be a "tomboy" early on, but as a teenager outdoor adventures I longed for were silently labeled "boys only." It's very important for families to talk about these issues, and for girls to be alert to who they really are. Reading about women like Rachel Carson and Amelia Earhart can help.

Pamela Alexander's second book of poems, *Commonwealth of Wings*, is written in the first person describing the life of John James Audubon—one way of "being a man" and exploring the natural world freely.

Agha Shahid Ali (Kashmir and Massachusetts) / It is so self-evident that people should be absolutely equal that it doesn't even occur to me to make a distinction. On a personal level, it is a nonissue. People should be free to realize themselves to the fullest.

Naomi: Despite a restless night filled with dreams of lobster battles, I have rushed to my computer this morning in order to get these poems and lists of pairs to you. What do you think?

Alise Alousi (Michigan) / Two thoughts on gender:
   (a) My mother gave me my name. That is what gave me my first voice. That voice sometimes still speaks for a girl in the back of the classroom or asleep on a roof in a country far away. It is about not being afraid of a voice or a name.
   (b) It is about fighting with boys and having them pull your skirt up.

Christianne Balk (Washington) / Christianne Balk grew up in upstate New York, where she enjoyed exploring the foothills of the Helderburg Mountains with her Welsh pony, Copper Dust, and her Labrador retriever, Indy.

Wendy Barker (Texas) / I believe that we can all cook together—enter the great soup together—such a rich and various broth, soup, sea—such a foaming and feeding stew.

Judith Barrington (Oregon) / Judith Barrington grew up in England, trying to fathom the mysteries of becoming a "proper woman." "The Dyke with No Name," who appears in several of her poems, is the character she created to tell about her own journey from the pain and fear to the eventual celebration of being a lesbian.

Linda Besant (Oregon) / I remember, as a child, running to my room in tears as my father and brother went camping and fishing. I had to stay home with my mother. Now, I go camping and keep house, race around on in-line skates, and write poetry, and work to make this a society where people can follow the call of their hearts.

Chana Bloch (California) / I was brought up to sit pretty, to smile for the camera, to keep my shoes polished and my legs crossed—the accomplishments of a sweet young thing. Now I'm discovering that my life can be as large as my imagination. It's not always easy—but these days, if something is hard, that's one more reason I am drawn to do it.

Robert Bly (Minnesota) / Robert Bly has been an important force in American letters since the 1950s and his translations of writers from other countries are among the finest. He is perhaps most widely known for *Iron John: A Book About Men* which was on *The New York Times* best seller list for sixty-five weeks. Each summer he runs the Conference on the Great Mother and the New Father.

Naomi: Hello? I haven't yet received any reactions to the poems I sent you. Have you gone on vacation? How come you never answer a question until I ask it more than three times? Is this a boy thing? Fill me in, bud.

George Bogin (New York) / George Bogin (1920-1988) was the author of *In a Surf of Strangers* and a book-length translation *Selected Poems and Reflections on the Art of Poetry*, by the Franco-Uruguayan writer, Jules Sepervielle.

Paul Bonin-Rodriguez (Texas) / I'm waiting for a nonmacho male superhero. They could call him SissyMan, and he could save the world from identity crises and lead the way for women presidents and men who allow themselves to cry in public and be affectionate with each other and feel okay about it. As long as he was true to his feelings, I wouldn't mind if he dated Batman or Wonder Woman.

Robin Boody Galguera (California) / Like most kids in America, my brother and I knew there were certain "boy things" and certain "girl things." We must have resisted those boundaries because Michael learned to cook and I learned about V-8 engines. Now both of us can concoct gourmet dinners and wrench on our cars.

Philip Booth (Maine) / Philip Booth's recent book of poems is called *Pairs* and focuses on "how singularly, plurally, selfishly, or generously, selves and pairs come to terms with each other, themselves, and their aging lives."

Rhonda Bower (Indiana) / Growing up on a farm allowed me the opportunity to be involved in activities and chores that typically involved boys. I helped bale hay and straw; helped plant corn, soybeans, and wheat; helped build and mend fences; helped take care of livestock; and participated on a livestock-judging team.

Robert Burlingame (Texas) / I have never found the consciousness of gender to be anything but liberating. Masculine and feminine necessities are woven, as they have to be, into all of us. But judging from what I see on TV, women and children are particularly endangered almost anywhere in our world now. So I tend to go along with what Adrienne Rich has said about the failure of patriarchal politics in this century.

Michael Burns (Missouri) / My gender consciousness changed in 1985, when my daughter was born. I had always been a supporter of equal rights for women, but thinking about my daughter's future, I realized how important her right to a full life would be to both of us.

Paul: To show you that I have not completely lost my mind, I submit the following list of possible pairs . . . I have not looked at your list since it arrived. I wanted to make my own initial choices independently.

Jacinto Jesús Cardona (Texas) / In my Mexican-American community, I noticed that "hombres" cast a shadow, and "las mujeres" lived in those shadows. Should a woman step out of her man's shadow, she was tagged "una Juana Gallo," Jane the Rooster.

Andrea Carlisle (Oregon) / When I was growing up, girls were supposed to wear patent leather shoes and velveteen dresses. Most of the time I liked to wear flannel shirts, corduroy pants, and sneakers. But sometimes I wore velveteen and patent leather because I thought it was fun and interesting to try everything. I still do.

When I write I am no one and nothing. I don't have a gender. I don't know what time it is, or what year. I can write as a man or as a woman. Writing is the one experience I have where I'm completely free.

Lucia Casalinuovo (Italy and California) / During my high school years, my father would lock me into the house once in a while and shout that women belong in the fields, not in school. Nevertheless, I finished high school, went to college, and became a teacher.

Nina Cassian (Romania and New York) / I believe there are differences between men and women on the physical level. Those differences do not affect or limit either creative or intellectual capacities.

Rosemary Catacalos (Texas and California) / When I was twelve years old, my adored paternal grandfather, a Greek immigrant, arranged my future marriage to a friend's grandson in Greece. Fortunately, my father was able to deter his dad, but the shock of firsthand discovery that men in many times and cultures have felt entitled to order "their" women's lives has never left me or my work.

Eric Chock (Hawaii) / I grew up with three sisters, and although I never thought of it before, maybe that's why I spent a lot of time alone, wandering in streams. My sisters never stayed out late; but I did, suffering the consequences of "The Belt."

Tom Clark (California) / The common fate of sentient beings sharing a fragile planet should be a matter for the exercise of compassionate understanding. I was brought up to believe boys and girls, women and men, are all human, and deserve the respect befitting that status. But things have changed, and it seems to me that in our haste to drive divisive wedges of "interest," "power," and "rights" between us, we've become like

Naomi: Fine, but I really, really think we should begin weighing the gloom factor. Are we going overboard with poems about death and loss and goneness? Are we too nostalgic? Is this what we get from being middle-aged parents with young children? Help!

creatures in a fairy tale, caught up in a terrible spell that blinds us to everything true. We're asking all the wrong questions: What makes people different from one another? What drives them apart? Why not ask: What do people have in common? What brings them together? Is there anything we can do to reconcile our differences and heal the pain of our several separations?

David Clewell (Missouri) / When I was seven years old, I barrelled into The Wrong Restroom at Colonial Farms restaurant in Middlebush, New Jersey. Very quickly I would learn that, while the *Women's* was more comfortably (even opulently) furnished, the line at the *Men's* was mercifully shorter.

Lucille Clifton (Maryland) / "We are a family of strong women and weak men," my father always told us, which was not helpful to my brother in his life at all. It also, I think, was an unfair burden to my sister and myself; always to be strong, whether we wanted to or not. Even in praise, such responsibility!

Christopher Cokinos (Kansas) / My awareness of gender issues didn't really take hold until I was a young adult in college. That's when I started writing seriously. Reading and writing helps me to take my blinders off. Until recently, I didn't think about how my family both conformed to and defied cultural norms. If I'd had the chance to read a book like this when I was a teenager, I might have been able to open up a dialogue with each of my parents sooner than I did—and that conversation might have changed the course of our lives in a positive way.

Julie M. Convisser (Oregon) / When I was a child, my older brother seemed godlike, able to do anything. Is a sister born who does not as a child blindly follow her big brother, thinking, "Me too?" Then one day, she knows she must find her own path. From that day forward, if she follows, it is to honor him.

Cathy Young Czapla (Vermont) / My father was a carpenter, and for me it was almost magical the way he could build things out of almost nothing. I wanted to be a carpenter, but I was born in 1950, and for a girl it wasn't an option. My father died three years ago of bone cancer, from the effects of being in Nagasaki during the war. There's a certain sadness in the poem because of that, seeing everything he had built fall apart and wanting to carry on the tradition. My son is nineteen now, and he can be anything he wants to be. So could a girl that age, which is wonderful.

Paul: Speak for yourself, kiddo. I'm showing off my new font. **Peace, baby!**

Andra R. Davis (Texas) / It bothered me at an early age to have to wear a shirt, to be told I "hit like a girl," that I had "no sense of direction." Yet I find it easier to conform outwardly to the cultural expectations of womanhood. I try not to conform inwardly—to live without anger, resentment, and to form my own opinions, aims, desires. I'm sure I'm not nearly as self-defined as I would like to think. My identity is inextricably intertwined with masculine expectations—father, lover, male mentors.

William Virgil Davis (Texas) / The mysteries of gender consciousness and the intrinsic differences between men and women are at the heart of "January." The final sentence of this prose poem implies the questions inherent in these mysteries between the sexes.

Toi Derricotte (Maryland and Pennsylvania) / All writers explore issues by which they are deeply affected. To me the most deeply affecting feelings are feelings of separation, isolation, and/or alienation. Race and gender often precipitate such moments of painful self-awareness.

We are all wounded by racism and sexism, but for some of us those wounds have been anesthetized. Writing can be a way of reclaiming those anesthetized parts of the self.

Jeannette Doob (Oregon) / As the son of Italian immigrants, my brother knew the freedom of riding his bike beyond the familiar streets of our neighborhood, but I knew the intimacy of my mother's kitchen and the joy of listening to women's voices turning reckless in a way they never did when men were around.

Moshe Dor (Israel) / Growing up in the years before Israel became a state, my family and my immediate community were deeply influenced by an ideology that formally embraced as a tenet of faith the equality of man and woman. This was the beacon held by both the youth movement and the underground to which I belonged. Only age and experience have made me aware of the gaps existing then and now between ideals and reality.

Rita Dove (Virginia) / When I was growing up, getting a superior education was a priority for all children, except that girls weren't pushed quite as hard. I thought I

Naomi: Is "The Skokie Theater" too wild? I mean, they're twelve years old! And whereas this may have happened for others of us at a later age, (twenty-five for me . . . just kidding!) doesn't the "moment of awakening" seem exquisitely wrought and universal in this poem? Hirsch says, "I didn't know one thing about the body yet, / about the deep foam filling my bones, / but I wanted to cry out in desolation"—you know, this poem made me cry out, just reading it! "I remember!" I love that the last word of "The Skokie Theater" is "changed." Isn't that what happens for boys and girls when they discover one another's—attraction? Nothing is the same, forever. What do you think?

wanted to study law; when college came around and I decided to become a poet instead, my parents swallowed hard but didn't raise a fuss. I'd like to believe that they supported me; even back then, however, I suspected I might have prompted more resistance if I had been a male, expected to support a family. So it happened that in one of fate's delicious ironic twists, gender stereotypes actually gave me the freedom to pursue the vocation of my dreams.

Denise Duhamel (Pennsylvania) / Brought up in a Catholic family, I wanted very much to be an altar boy, not hearing the word *boy* in the description. No one could console me when I was told I was not qualified—not my parents or the priests, none of whom had a good explanation. Even though I didn't know what feminists were back then, in third grade I became one.

Paul Durcan (Ireland) / Some of Durcan's book titles are *Daddy, Daddy, Crazy About Women*, and *A Snail in My Prime*. It has been said of his work, "For him poetry is storytelling and his stories are told in a direct fashion that make them totally accessible." (Roger McGough)

Cornelius Eady (New York) / In the black, working-class/low-income neighborhood where I grew up, the idea of being creative or trying to get an education was sometimes looked upon as *sissified*, if one was male, or as trying to act male if one was a woman. If I have one hope, it's that my work as a teacher and poet helps to contribute to the breaking down of those stubborn beliefs.

Gunnar Ekelöf (Sweden) / Gunnar Ekelöf wrote poems influenced by modern music as well as mythology and mysticism. His translator, Robert Bly, has written that Ekelof is "an uncomfortable poet; he tries to make the reader conscious of lies, and of the unstable and shifty nature of the human ego."

George Eklund (Kentucky) / The issue of gender has always carried significant weight in our culture. It is my hope that future generations will explore and celebrate the complexities of gender rather than allowing themselves to act upon or be acted upon by restrictive notions of what it means to be male or female.

Sharif S. Elmusa (Palestine and Washington D.C.) / I have been happily transformed into a modern male. I spend many hours every week in the kitchen. I love stuffing

---

Paul: I'd like to back up a little and look at what comes before "changed." The "lovesick" couple is "gripping/each other's hand, trembling." For me, those words capture the essence of that point in life, no matter when it comes.

vegetables, zucchinis, eggplants, peppers. I stuff them with rice, spice, nuts and minced—you've got it—machismo.

Gevorg Emin (Armenia) / Gevorg Emin, son of teachers, was born in 1919. He graduated from the Polytechnic Institute as a hydraulic engineer when his first book of poetry was published. He now has thirty volumes of poetry and has won every top literary award in the former Soviet Union. His sister is a poet and his brother is a composer.

His translator, Diana Der Hovanessian, was told by her own father, "You can be anything you choose." Although she is now working on an anthology of poems by Armenian women, she does not think poems have gender.

Robert Farnsworth (Maine) / Early on, though I wasn't yet sure that boys could be boys in many ways, I knew that there were many kinds of girls. There was pale, brainy Regina, with whom I drew pictures next door in the shade. And there was Caroline, my loud, tanned, long-haired cousin, much to be admired for the tick that once lodged behind her knee. They both colored better than I did.

Edward Field (New York) / My poetry speaks for the unloved and unwanted, because of the rejection I felt, growing up, from teachers and other kids, who treated me badly for being Jewish, undersized, and what they called a sissy, and also from my parents who didn't understand and protect me.

Karen Fiser (California) / At this time, when people seem to focus only on what divides the people of the world—gender, race, nationality, religious affiliation, sexual preference—I am trying, in my work and in my life, to speak about and honor what brings us together. Is this not one main task of the poet, to give voice to our common humanity?

Tess Gallagher (Washington) / I enjoy noticing how much freedom and grace is coming to both men and women, as they honor each other.

Reginald Gibbons (Texas and Illinois) / I grew up in Texas, where the measure of a boy—especially in the eyes of men, everybody's fathers, other boys—was sports and hunting. But what were the other ways that a boy could win the deep admiration of other kids, and adults, too? I don't think I was very good at finding them. But I know they exist. My best friends liked talking and music. We began reading books for our-

---

Naomi: Let's pair "The Skokie Theater" with Anna Swir's "Angel" poem. Connect it to her "astounded / to the very blood" description. Yes! Her poem is simpler, more suggestive, less descriptive, but equivalent in its daze. Do you agree? And you sent me the rather mysterious "Spoon." Do you think "Spoon" is a love poem?

selves, and we thought about, and dreamed about, the world beyond where we lived. I loved running across a field, but was slow. I loved reading a novel, and was fast. I loved thinking about things, sometimes to myself, sometimes with others, and that was the most amazing race of them all. And, in this race, running alongside me, were girls as well as boys. Knowing everything a boy could do, everything a girl could do, is so much more exciting than listening to people say what a boy or girl can't do.

Jack Gilbert (California) / Being seen as a male helped to give shape to my sense of myself in somewhat the same way that being an American (rather than a member of some other culture) did. Certainly there are differences—physically, for sure. And possibly other more subtle ways that could make the world richer and more interesting. As to my poetry, the central concern is romantic love, which is largely the result of the "otherness" of each gender for the other. . . .

Sandra M. Gilbert (California) / When I was growing up, I didn't think about the differences gender might make in my life, though I now realize many of my dreams and wishes had to do with wanting to be a successful *girl* rather than just a successful person. I'm sure I worried more about my looks than a boy my age might have, and had more fantasies about being popular. After I graduated from college and got out into the so-called "real world," I began to understand more about the social and cultural obstacles I had to face just because I was female. Eventually I started writing essays and poems about gender pressures in general and the experiences of women in particular. I've coauthored a number of books with my close friend Susan Gubar (including *The Madwoman in the Attic: The Woman Writer and the Nineteenth-Century Literary Imagination* and the three-volume *No Man's Land: The Place of the Woman Writer in the Twentieth Century*), and we've coedited the *Norton Anthology of Literature by Women*.

Maria Mazziotti Gillan (New Jersey) / When I was growing up in an Italian-American community, my family believed that a girl should be either a first-grade teacher or a secretary because these jobs were respectable and could be held until she married. When I informed my parents that I wanted to be a writer, my cousin, the accountant, and the only other person in my family to go to college, said that was one of the most impractical ambitions he had ever heard of. My mother insisted I had to get a degree in liberal arts. I refused to go to a teacher's college. The battle was long and intense, but I finally won.

Paul: Amigo! Stop with the poems already! They are only complicating things for me at this point! I need wood for the fire. I need to shovel the driveway. For me an anthology reaches a point where it needs shape. I think we're at that point.

My parents acted out of their love for me and their desire to protect me. I have tried to raise my daughter to have the freedom I was not given. I have been shocked sometimes to discover how much of my upbringing is still so much a part of me. I want her to be free, but this little old lady in black seems to live inside me. She is my mother and all the other old ladies who congregated on the front stoops of Paterson. I have to stop her from making me afraid.

Albert Goldbarth (Illinois and Kansas) / I don't believe that a real poem is so one-ply thin as to be "about gender" (or race, or religion, etc.) any more than (if the hubris can be pardoned here) *Moby Dick* is a fish story; if anything, I'd like to think that real poems are true enough to the rich complexity of being alive that they rise above such Oprah-like talk show inanity.

M. Eliza Hamilton (Illinois) / Being a Woman is about death and rebirth—the life cycle of the universe. This body is the Creator's gift to help us understand the beginning and ending of things and the connection of all things/people to each other. To know this is to look at each thing/person as a fragment of mySelf. To accept this is to love mySelf and all things reflected in that Self.

Lois Marie Harrod (New Jersey) / As "The Fitting Room" suggests, it was important to me to give my daughter choices that I wasn't given, choices that would protect her independence and sense of self. As a high school teacher, I know how easy it is for young women to dress literally and figuratively for others and to lose their freedom.

Penny Harter (New Mexico) / A male poet friend praised my book *Grandmother's Milk* saying, "Only women can write about the body so dearly and soulfully." I wonder. Other women's poems about female and family experience have helped inspire my own, including several in my book *Shadow Play* (Simon & Schuster Books for Young Readers).

James Hathaway (Arizona) / I distinctly remember feeling confused at age five or six about why the boys were on one side of the playground and the girls on the other. Weren't we all the same except for the clothes we wore and the length of our hair? I know now, of course, that there are differences, and deep ones, but it still seems to me that the only distinctions that really matter are those, say, between me and a bird, me and a cat, us and the earth, us and the sky (and everything above and below it). A question: If someone seems strange to us, is it we or they who are not human? I know very few people (male or female) who are stranger to me than a tree.

Naomi: Eyes too full? Loosen up, buddy. I'm sorry to say I DO have to send you a few more poems today whether you like it or not. YOU NEED TO SEE THESE AND I HADN'T FOUND THEM YESTERDAY.

Samuel Hazo (Pennsylvania) / Anybody who writes anything worth anything doesn't think in terms of gender, but in terms of personality. One of the tragic aspects of modern culture is that men are regarded as the natural enemies of women, and women as the natural enemies of men. I can't think of anything more sterile than that. I believe Plato was right when he said that we started out as one being and were split into two. If you look at any one person today you'll see that they are incomplete, sexually incomplete. . . . We need each other to be whole.

Christine Hemp (New Mexico) / I grew up a tomboy—playing baseball, climbing birch trees, and riding horses. After college I worked as a carpenter. Life is too brief to limit what men and women can be for one another, and a poet is fed by many kinds of pleasure: fly-fishing, herb gardening, cooking, and kissing.

Judith Hemschemeyer (Florida) / Because I am a woman, things happen to me that only happen to women. I write about these things—childbirth, for instance. But many of the things I experienced as a child—the feeling of being an intermediary between mother and father in the poem in this book, for example—could as well have happened to a boy. And the girl in the poem becomes, in the mind of the adult writing the poem, the male god Mercury.

Zbigniew Herbert (Poland) / In his late teens, Herbert fought in the underground resistance against the Nazis. Later he studied law, economics, and philosophy. He has described himself as "the poet of a certain age, in the middle of an uncertain age."

B. Vincent Hernandez (Texas) / I live with my "husband," Tom. I think it's a shame that we can't be truly married just because we are men. "Sunday" represents just one possibility for the roles that men and women play in our society, and I do not believe we should judge others merely on the basis of gender.

Geof Hewitt (Vermont) / I've been writing poems since I was seventeen years old— I'm now in my fifties. My latest book, *Just Worlds*, takes its title from "Typographical Errors." The poem is a joke; the title and last word of the poem are the setup and the punch line, respectively. Because the poem is a joke and has little or nothing to do with the focus of *I Feel a Little Jumpy Around You*, I think it's a joke that it is included. Nevertheless, I am honored!

Paul: I'm ankle deep in poems and fax scrolls. You owe me five bucks. The other day we couldn't find Emma. Turned out she was buried under your recent poem deluge. I'm pretty poemed out, kiddo. I think we have a book. All we need to do is decide which poems it will hold.

Conrad Hilberry (Michigan) / Though the poem doesn't say for sure, I think of the speaker in "Spoon" as a female. Do other readers hear the voice that way? In any case, a number of my poems are written from a woman's point of view, and I value the liberty to try that. Who would want to write, always, as an aging white male?

Edward Hirsch (Texas) / When I was in high school I fell for poetry the same way I fell for my first girlfriend—with a wild exhilaration bordering on terror. The feeling for poetry didn't go away.

Linda Hogan (Colorado) / In my poetry, the major influence is not gender so much as nature and questions and explorations of human spirit. However, in my fiction, my characters are primarily women and girls, the relationships between women, and a concern with the emotional and spiritual health of women who are whole in their world, and attuned to the natural world.

David Huddle (Vermont) / One of my ten books is about writing. The other nine are about gender. I keep hoping to conquer my ignorance.

Albert Huffstickler (Texas) / I was raised in a family where my father was head of the household and had final decisions even when he was wrong. At the time I was growing up—I'm sixty-seven now—women pretty much were housewives, nurses, or schoolteachers. It took a while for things to dawn on me, but I now consider myself a feminist. I think that women have the same rights as men in terms of job, salary, how they want to lead their lives. I don't really think the genders are exactly alike. God forbid! I will never, for example, be so enlightened that I will go to a man for a certain kind of tenderness and support. I don't want women to become *like* men. I just want them to have the same freedom and opportunity as men.

Gary Hyland (Canada) / A teen in the late fifties–early sixties, I was aware enough to be troubled by the misogyny of my friends and me. I really wanted to believe girls were people, though the cyclonic effect they had on me was an impediment. Today, a supporter of all but extreme feminism, I am troubled by the vestigial sexism I acquired as a teen.

Naomi: Upon rereading our text, I think we have many more lighthearted (intelligently funny) poems than I originally thought. Sometimes the pairing makes them even funnier than they were on their own. I feel quite feverish on this home stretch. Sometimes when I am sitting on my floor putting these poems together, it seems electrical charges are leaping out of the pages. Still, you may feel free to challenge my (luminous) couples. Do you think "Spoon" is a love poem?

David Ignatow (New York) / David Ignatow wrote in a poem called "Nice Guy," "I had a friend and he died. Me. / I forgot to mourn him that busy day / earning a living." Many of his urban-based poems examine the ways men and women spend their time, and have titles like "Brief Cases" and "Self-Employed." His daughter Yaedi, who grew up listening to both her parents' typewriters clicking away, is also a contributor to this collection.

Yaedi E. Ignatow (Arizona) / The higher Self has no gender, and is, after all, the place where inspired, illumined poetry has come from—from both female and male "ecstatic" poets down through the centuries. Joy between friends comes from celebrating what we have in common. To create peace in the world, we must do the same. Not that we should ignore injustice, but choose our battles and look within. Each struggle will challenge our ability to retain our peaceful state while executing right action. This is one more thing as difficult for one sex to do as for the other.

Cill Janeway (Massachusetts) / One of the things that affected me most about growing up female was the mixed messages about our bodies. If I could say anything to young women growing up today, it is that your bodies are beautiful how ever they grow and however they change.

Phyllis Janowitz (New York) / Are there intrinsic differences between men and women? I think that evolutionary pressures have often made it imperative for women and men to solve problems in antipodal ways. But barriers that might be linguistically insurmountable can, at times, be overcome by the intensity of reproductive urges.

Paulette Jiles (Missouri, Canada, and Texas) / North Spirit, a recent memoir by Jiles, describes her years working for the Canadian Broadcasting Corporation in a remote Ontario village. "I thought I had brought all I needed to survive in a lonely cabin in the great north woods. I had a hurricane lamp, and scented kerosene, packages of caramels and People of the Deer, pink cotton sheets, a mirror and matches, and four or five blank notebooks. If I had been able to obtain a silver tea service and a twill ulster, I would have brought those too. . . . My models of choice had always been those intrepid Englishwomen who explored places in the world remote from themselves and their cultures, Lady Isabella Bird and Edith Durham, Freya Stark; ladies who stalked off into the Interior with hairpins and changes of sheets, cranky old maids with rare dictionaries and letters of credit. One could do worse."

Paul: It's in the single digits here and much lower with the howling wind. We're talking nose hairs sticking and your throat closing up when you suck in the frigid air. Oh, how I long for the San Antonio Cowboy Breakfast.

Roger Jones (Texas) / I've always envied women for their sensitivity and their remarkable perceptiveness to nuance and subtlety. Particularly growing up in Texas, which still subscribes thoroughly to a macho ethic, I've found the sensitivity of females an admirable trait.

Diane Hina Kahanu (Hawaii) / When my mother was working, she thought my older sister was watching over me, but I was really with my older brother, catching crabs in the swamp or red fish in the ocean. I was and am a tomboy. I used to pray to God at night that I'd wake up a boy. I wanted, still want, a boy's freedom.

Jane Kenyon (New Hampshire) / Jane Kenyon died of leukemia at the age of forty-seven in 1995. For the last twenty years of her life she lived with her husband, the poet Donald Hall, on a farm in New Hampshire. Her *Otherwise: New & Selected Poems* appeared in 1996.

Kathryn Kerr (Illinois) / Men and women, boys and girls, were treated very differently when I was growing up. I was never satisfied with the limited experiences allotted me. I now teach my biology students that humans have forty-six chromosones. For men and women, forty-five are identical. We are more *human* than male or female, more alike than different.

Miriam Kessler (Pennsylvania) / Imagining a person who epitomizes my own gender, I think: Amelia Earhart! Free, a woman, doing whatever she wanted to do! I, a child of her era, wanted such freedom, too. But I was told that "children should be seen and not heard." Earhart was my heroine then and now, along with other women who have dared.

Faye Kicknosway (Hawaii) / The "female" thing did and has, and probably for always, who can know, shorten who I was or could become. So said my entire family, who lived close to the law of pink and blue, the right and wrong way. The arts, imagination, were the hole through that confinement into the work of making me up, which is what I still do; a little from here, from there, the part marked blue only, and mostly. To bounce, be curious, be forthright, to do, be active, make up a world, that has been said to be "man's work." No, no; mine too, thank you.

What I can, how I can write/draw are maps I have spent my life reworking. To be imaginative is to break rules, to leap across, to see and act. It is making up what

---

Naomi: I'm ready to kick out all poems we don't really love. I'm ready to kick out all poems that don't light up the page. Please fax the "Cow" poem again, which keeps running off to graze in our warm winter-green meadows.

hasn't been there before! Not all "pink" "blue" separate, but mixed together, a whole personality.

Galway Kinnell (Vermont and New York) / My mother, who came from Ireland, was a knower. My father, a carpenter from Scotland, was a maker. I learned how to make more quickly than I learned how to know, and so, as I grew up, my mother had more to teach me than my father. It was the same when I started writing: I had more to learn from my mother in poetry, Emily Dickinson, who wrote of the emotions, than I did from my father in poetry, Walt Whitman, who wrote of the world around us. Without both sets of parents inside me, I could never have been a poet.

Ron Koertge (California) / Gender affects my writing less in poetry than in prose. The poem in this anthology has a female angle, but it's not really gender specific; we've all longed after someone, or worse, for Love. In my young adult fiction, though, I've tried and failed to write a novel from a girl's point of view.

I'm urged to write as a male in order to attract the elusive boy-reader.

Ted Kooser (Nebraska) / I believe that women make better poets than men because they are, generally, less competitive and less likely to make elaborate displays of style and attitude. Men can't seem to avoid acting like young roosters.

Melody Lacina (California) / When I was growing up, girls were taught to be kinder and quieter than boys, and to cover up our intelligence. It took me years to learn that keeping still isn't good for anybody's head or heart. Now I know you have to trust your voice and use it.

Margo LaGattuta (Michigan) / When I was young and wanted to be a writer, I was told by some of my teachers, "Don't worry about a job. You're just going to marry and have babies, anyway." Society didn't seem to value me for my mind. Now my babies are grown, and I write poems like "I Vacuum, Therefore I Am" to set the record straight.

Kurtis Lamkin (Pennsylvania) / I have recently completed a recording of praise-poems called "My Juju." I play the Kors, a twenty-one-stringed West African instrument, and have performed in many music and poetry festivals.

Paul: You can write poems about anything. As I thumb through our manuscript I see how true that is. "Tomatoes!" Or—take a look at "Cow Worship" with "Cow" by Joan Fern Shaw. What a delightful pair. Stern is playful, in the here and now. Shaw is more reflective as she uses the cow to recall a childhood experience.

James Laughlin (New York) / I don't think that gender questions apply to this poem. If you look at it you'll see it's about problems of the generation gap.

Li-Young Lee (Illinois) / The voice in the poem is important to me, since it is the identity of a possible self. And though the subject matter of a poem may involve distinctions in gender, and though the drama of a poem may unfold between distinct figures with gender, the voice I'm always trying to hear, in which I'm trying to speak, is anonymous: without gender, without allegiance, without country, without issue.

Fay Lipshitz (Israel) / I grew up in a very conservative environment—South Africa in the 50s and 60s—where people were defined, and defined themselves, by race, language, religion, and gender. It took me many years to liberate myself from these attitudes.

Joan Logghe (New Mexico) / As above, so below, or as in macrocosm, so in micro-cosm. Or, if we can't get along with each other, how can we have global peace? I think men and women need to make peace, just as sure as countries. Some days I think men and women are worlds apart and in a marriage, it is sacred to find common ground. My writing is often about making peace with my husband. We are both impossible to get along with, yet love curls through the armor of gender or being right, and writing is my particular sword.

Robert Long (New York) / Relationships I've had often enter my poems, but it's really more a matter of being haunted by someone and trying to capture something of the feeling of that relationship on the page than a matter of thinking about gender. The poem in this book happens to be about a guy I knew, but it might as well have been about a girl, at least as far as the reader is concerned.

Phillip Lopate (Brooklyn) / I came from a family with very strong women—two sisters and a mother—who took no guff from the men in the family (my father, my older brother, and me). My mother particularly had the tendency to go out and get what she wanted out of life, whereas my father's character was to be a dutiful worker. I'm a little of both: at times a plodding worker, at other times willful and a butterfly. I've written all kinds of things—novels, poetry collections, and books of personal essays. I believe in honesty and telling it like it is, the way my outspoken mother does, and in the great pleasures of craft and good work habits, which I learned from my father.

Naomi: I still think "Step on His Head" by James Laughlin is one of the most tender, memorable poems I've ever read. After reading it aloud for years, it still gives me a chill.

Wing Tek Lum (Hawaii) / No fig leaves. I wish to celebrate my maleness (whatever that means), just as I hope women will celebrate femaleness. Only then can the opposite sexes truly be able to know and love one another; conversely (following Jesus' Golden Rule) only by interactions with the other sex can one truly learn what it means to be of a particular gender.

George Ella Lyon (Kentucky) / Since my first name is George, people often expect me to be male. At church camp I got assigned to the boy's cabin. At the music festival the judge insisted that I was a substitute for myself. Such experiences made me very aware of gender. And words.

Gary Margolis (Vermont) / I went to college as a three-sport athlete and graduated as a poet and an athlete. I found a way to let the artist under my football pads write himself into this world of images, music, and experience that, in the garden, was first and still is *hers*.

Chuck Martin (Washington) / Chuck Martin's poem "Size Is Relative" appeared as part of a poems-in-buses project in Seattle where it was read by both men and women.

Khaled Mattawa (New Jersey) / Whenever we had visitors in Libya, where I grew up, the men and women sat in separate rooms. I sat with the men and listened to them talk about work and money. There were stretches of unbearable silence, and very little laughter. As soon as I found it appropriate to leave the room, I darted to where my mother entertained her visitors. The women cried and consoled each other, told amusing stories, talked about their relatives and in-laws. I sat with the women as long as my mother allowed me. Sometimes I stood outside the door listening to the women, never wanting to go back to join the men, dreading the year when I would be too old to sit and hear my mother and her visitors chat.

Jane Mayhall (New York) / I've never been troubled by gender-related problems. Being a writer, I always felt I had as strong a chance at self-realization as Walt Whitman and George Eliot. My poem "Tracing Back" alludes to historical injustices. But the characters are living people, the mother and father are not enemies of each other, but forced to live in the prison of other people's limited attitudes. In personal life, my parents encouraged me and my brother to get an education and to fight for what we believed. My mother was an intuitive "feminist" without ever having heard the word.

Paul: Once again, the telltale red smear along the edge of my fax paper tells me that (another) roll of paper is ending. Sigh.

My father was proud of my career and achievements. In a true culture, gender would seem an outmoded, outlandish concept.

Walter McDonald (Texas) / I loved playing baseball, and still love the game. As an Air Force pilot, I loved flying, and the skies still thrill me. I played ball and flew with guys, but, I realized, always *for* girls—and I married the girl of my dreams. Sportsmanship seemed in both games a decent but thin veneer for the sobering fact that competition always means survival of the fittest.

Richard E. McMullen (Michigan) / Boys could write things, but poems had to be rhymed humor. Serious poems were something girls did. I wrote my first one in my twenties.

W. S. Merwin (Pennsylvania and Hawaii) / W. S. Merwin has written poems his whole lifetime that explore and penetrate identity and being—not only that of humans, but also of animals, places, plants, and consciousness itself. In an early poem called "For Now," he wrote, "I grew up in the rooms of the rain."

Linda Meyers (Washington) / I identify very strongly as a woman writer, and have drawn much of my material from childhood memories of my parents, who had a traditional marriage. Others of my poems respond to my adult situations as wife, mother, and artist.

E. Ethelbert Miller (Washington, D.C.) / We should all strive for oneness . . . John Coltrane playing "A Love Supreme" is a reminder of who we are. All men and women are divine.

E. K. Miller (Oregon) / When I was growing up, the work in our home was totally divided according to sex: The boys took care of the animals and the barn, and my sister and I cleaned the house and did the cooking. But we all worked together in the garden; we spent most summer days planting, weeding, and picking vegetables. I hated every second of it. Of course, now I have a big garden of my own—and I love it! Go figure.

Jim Wayne Miller (Kentucky) / Whether it's an intrinsic difference or not, I don't know. But I think men tend to compete while women cooperate. Men turn something

---

Naomi: Don't you think this Nellie Wong poem "Where Are You Going?" is an absolute must? Think how many lives are in it! How many reverberations and echoes of history, someone trying to get someone else to do what they want for some reason of their own! I like how, even after all the prodding, it ends up with an accusation. "Stranger, stranger, stranger." And yet the voice sounds so eerily familiar! No stranger at all.

quiet and meditative, like fishing, into a tournament! That's stupid! I wish men were more like women in the tendency to cooperate.

Karen Mitchell (Mississippi) / My greatest ambition as a child was to be a writer and publish a book of poetry. I began writing poetry at the age of twelve, and won my first literary contest while in high school.

Nora Mitchell (Vermont) / I went to a high school that actively encouraged girls. When I went away to college, a school that had just gone coed, I found myself in an environment where women were newcomers and in the minority. Sometimes we were welcomed, but at other times resented and scorned. Team sports provided relief and freedom. We could be tough, competitive, sweaty, and crude, and no one could care less.

Thylias Moss (Michigan) / There were no limits; my parents both worked inside and outside the home according to their abilities and interests. They gave me: submarine, steamroller, Chatty Cathy doll to say *I love you* when I pulled the string in her neck, paint to resore CC's washed-out smile. Girl was forceful.

Harryette Mullen (Alabama, Texas, and California) / Growing up in a female-centered household, I learned that women are strong and men are a mystery. I wish I knew more about the men in my family who were distant or who died too soon.

Eric Nelson (Georgia) / Growing up, I never made my bed, set the table, or did dishes—those were my sisters' chores. My job was to empty and clean the trashcans. It was many years before I even thought about how this division of labor affected my views of male and female roles in society.

Marilyn Nelson (Connecticut) / I grew up with the expectation that I would have a career, marry, and have children. I have fulfilled that expectation, sometimes with difficulty. It's hard to wear so many hats, to juggle so many balls, to be so many people. But my mother and grandmother, both of whom were teachers, were my role models, women who—though they probably yearned sometimes for escape—managed to do it all. I hope I do as well as they did.

Diana O'Hehir (California) / I'm very conscious of writing as a woman, maybe of trying to say to the other half of the human race, "This is how *we* see it!"

Paul: Yes, and think how this works with Cornelius Eady's poem "January," in which there's the line "If he catches her, / What will he lose?" Or "It will be another thing / We can't just quite put our fingers on, / A slight feeling / Of uneasiness . . ." In both poems there are people imagining "catching" other people.

Tommy Olofsson (Sweden) / Olofsson teaches, translates, writes as a critic for a Swedish newspaper, and lives with his wife and four daughters. His book *Elemental Poems*, translated by Jean Pearson, is available in the United States.

Peter Oresick / The tension between genders in the workplace is palpable. In this poem, I worked backwards from that tension to uncover the roots of it: in another place and time. Tension, friction, love.

Gregory Orfalea (California and Washington, D.C.) / My father epitomized for me what a man should be: strong in body and soul, and big of heart.

Gregory Orr (Virginia) / I see my poem as a series of metaphors and similes that dramatize the anguish of being a man. But they are not denunciations or self-denunciations—poetry, through its magic of imagination and rhythm, is inherently celebratory, and there is an element of celebration in this anguish. The great Greek poet Sappho invented a word: "bittersweet"—she used it to describe the spirit of many lyric poems, and I would be glad to think it applied to mine.

Grace Paley (Vermont) / One of Grace Paley's collections of stories was called *The Little Disturbances of Man, Stories of Men and Women At Love*. Another well-loved book of Paley's is called *Enormous Changes at the Last Minute*. It has been said of her writing, "I can't think of another writer who captures the itch of the city, love between parents and children, or the cutting edge of combat, as well." (Lis Harris, *The New York Times Book Review*)

Linda Pastan (Maryland) / My father wanted his only child, me, to follow in his footsteps and to become a doctor. I have always felt that it was because I was "only" a girl that he allowed me to go my own way.

When I got married, in the early 50s, a woman was expected to produce homemade desserts every night and perfectly ironed shirts. It took me ten years of silence to find the courage to go back to my real work: writing poetry again.

Naomi: Butterfly nets! Cages and traps! I've been thinking about that Mary Clark poem you sent me about the figs, which ends, "if you love me, get sick / on these with me." I put it off to the side but kept coming back to it. These poems are alive! How we want the people we love to do what we say . . . even if it's get sick on something, or have a fight when *we* feel like fighting. . . . She's the power figure in her poem, making the suggestions, while Gevorg Emin is the power figure in his, in the orchard. One thing I keep wondering about men and women involves empowerment and control—we all want to have the power to do what we want to do, but how does that affect our relationships with our closest people?

Raymond R. Patterson (New York) / I try very hard to overcome my narrow child-hood education regarding gender. A much younger sister, a wife, and a daughter are among women who help me as a mature adult.

Richard Peabody (Maryland) / My father was the Hemingway hero incarnate. He asked if I was gay when I began to write poetry. In his world, real men didn't waste valu-able hunting and gathering time on such frivolous endeavors as dreams, games, fan-tasies, or even movies. I will never understand why he and other macho men like him continue to view the arts as female and beneath them.

Molly Peacock (New York) / If I could have picked my chromosomes, I would have chosen the two x's that I have. I wrote my first poem in fifth grade, the grade I teach in the poem "Our Room." Writing the poem made me know I was telling the truth the way I saw it as a girl (even though boys could laugh at me, just as I fear in the poem). But liking to be who I was made me dare to tell that truth about my father. I felt that if I tried to say what really happened, everyone, boy or girl, would gain by it.

Marge Piercy (Massachusetts) / I was born a woman, so I am a feminist. That means I think it is rather fine to be a woman, but would be even finer if we could be assured of the same pay, if it were safe to walk down the street, if everyone didn't think our weight and appearance were public property like the weather, and if doctors and hospitals were more geared to our needs.

Andrea Potos (Wisconsin) / Exploring and "mining" the traditional details of women's lives in my poetry—whether it's putting on makeup, folding socks, or shaping cookie dough—has deepened my own appreciation of being a woman.

Alberto Ríos (Arizona) / In the 50s, we weren't just boys; we were the Vikings of America, and anybody could be one, but to join up you had to drink a can of lemon juice. We were just boys, however, if only by default; no girls really seemed interested in the lemon juice thing, though it took us years to figure out that this was what had kept us apart. It wasn't our parents at all.

Del Marie Rogers (Texas) / When I began publishing, it was difficult for a woman poet to get work published, even in magazines. I've never wanted to be a man, but it was impossible to accept the widely held belief that I could not be a woman and a poet.

Paul: I still get goose bumps over some of these poems and pairs.

William Pitt Root (New York) / As children, the difference between boys and girls is unbelievable; as teenagers, it's like, incredible; as grown-up men and women, it's increasingly laughable.

Liz Rosenberg (New York) / I have never trusted words like "gender." Growing up female, I was lucky to have a mother who encouraged me to be independent, a father whose ambitions for his daughters were unbounded, and a sister who led the way. All the same, I think there are expectations we get from the world around us, from movies, fairy tales, maybe the ozone—and I often find myself battling against myself, I mean, my sense of who I should be, and who I'm allowed to be. Are men and women different? I think so. Both sexes must try to get as free as they can.

Judy Ruiz (Missouri) / Gender was THE issue in my family and the community while I was growing up and it continues to affect everything I do, think, say, and write. My brother is affected also, and he had sex-change surgery five years ago—so he's my sister now. This has been very strange, especially for my children, and for the children my brother fathered before his surgery. It is precisely this sort of gender bewilderment that causes ME to come to my own mind as the one who epitomizes the gender "Woman." The epitome of "Man" is my partner. It's a big world. If I can't put my faith in the fact of my body, where can I put it?

Carole Satyamurti (England) / One of the poets I admire most is Elizabeth Bishop. She has a way of combining feeling, thought, and the use of language that seems to me to exemplify what good poetry—by either gender—is about.

The very best poets transcend the limitations of gender—limitations that tend to make men write poems that are merely clever, and women, poems that are merely expressions of feeling. I do think, though, that poetry by women is often under-valued because the influential readers (publishers, editors, critics) are men. I think male readers start from the assumption that the interesting writers are men, so female writers have an initial credibility gap to overcome.

Mary Jo Schimelpfenig (Washington) / When I was growing up, the neighborhood kids used to give me a bad time about not staying inside the lines when we colored. I've

---

Naomi: So do I. I was reading, for example, the combo by Kessler and Bogin, "All Their Names Were Vincent" and "Nineteen," and thinking about the perfect interweave of their scenes, how vividly they evoke a whole early era, staring at one another when the other isn't looking, the great magnetic field of longing . . . then both poems shoot forward into the present. Yet there are differences, too—in her poem, she says, "I do not miss them now," and in his, there's something more wistful at the end, don't you think? Don't you think the voice in his poem wishes he had done something differently?

come to see gender-related concepts like "masculine" and "feminine" as social constructs, big black lines on the pages of society's coloring book. I'm still aware of people who want me to stay within those gender lines, but I find it more rewarding to scribble right on past.

Philip Schultz (New York) / As a boy I looked up to and feared my father and loved my mother. Most or all good feelings were associated with women. Men were often frightening, abrupt. I fought with boys and courted—trusted—girls. These feelings hold, no doubt.

Charles Simic (Yugoslavia and New Hampshire) / I had received before your "illuminating gender issues" questions and ignored them. It's no point in my explaining to you that they are completely idiotic since I'm sure you and the editors are convinced that they're otherwise. Let's just say that I have no interest in answering them.

Naomi Stroud Simmons (Texas) / As a woman I have profited from the feminist movement even though I did not actively participate and disapproved of some of the changes. In retrospect, I cannot deny the great debt I owe to the ones who braved criticism to bring the changes we all enjoy.

Marylee A. Skwirz (Texas) / As a woman born in 1930, gender was predestination.

Edith Södergran (Finland) / Edith Södergran's early influences were the poets Goethe and Heine and she wrote first in German. Her parents were Swedish. Her favorite cat, Totti (often pictured in portraits with her) was disliked and ultimately shot by her next-door neighbors. She died at age thirty-one after a long struggle with tuberculosis. Her intensely visionary poems were often poorly received and misunderstood during her lifetime, though she is now considered Finland's greatest contemporary poet.

Kim R. Stafford (Oregon) / I learned from my six-year-old daughter that "a brain is a he, a body is a he or she, and a heart is a she," and also that "boys are strong, but girls remember better—that's fair, we each have one thing."

Paul: I love the way Bogin's narrator can't get himself to do what he wants to do. The last stanza is full of regret. You asked about the voice in Bogin's poem, but what about the speaker in Kessler's poem? She says, "I do not miss them now," but does she really mean it? I have my doubts. I think the thirty years of marriage have given her security, but I sense a longing for what Vincent, Ernie, and Paul might have given her.

William Stafford (Oregon) / William Stafford grew up in little towns in Kansas, and went on to become one of America's finest poets. In a poem called "A Girl Daddy Used to Know," he wrote, "you look back, and the stupid heart, too dumb, too honest, never gets lost." He was loyal to the honesty of childhood, and the power of poetry to champion that. He died in 1993.

Judith W. Steinbergh (Massachusetts) / Before I had my children, gender was not a significant factor in my writing. Once my children were born, I began to examine the expectations of the culture toward mothers, the images that arose out of domestic life, and the importance of documenting a woman's life with her family. "Letting the Parakeet Fly" places the muse in the home among the laundry, the plants, and the still things.

Gerald Stern (New Jersey, Iowa, and Pennsylvania) / Although I am seventy years old, I grew up with fairly advanced gender ideas. Women were honored, distinguished, and professional in my family in Europe and the United States. My true hero was Libby Barach, my maternal grandmother, who spoke six languages, was wise and beautiful, and loved me dearly.

There are obvious differences between men and women, which I love, but our spirits are exactly the same. So, therefore, are our dreams.

Ruth Stone (Vermont) / In my father's family were strong men and strong women—intellectuals, teachers, lawyers. My grandmother wrote and painted. My mother was musical. My father played drums. My mother's mother was a country woman—but I don't think she felt less than equal to others. It was the general culture that told me I was disadvantaged. I learned the sad truth about inequality from the world.

Anna Swir (Poland) / Anna Swir, who died in 1984, published poems renowned for their passion and feminism when she was over sixty. As a child, she said she was "terribly shy, ugly, and crushed by a mountain of complexes." However, as an older women, her translator, Czeslaw Milosz, described her as seeming "much stronger—in the physical sense too—than she had been in her youth: an attractive woman, lithe, with a ruddy complexion, her hair like the white mane of a fairy-tale witch."

Arthur Sze (New Mexico) / Thinking of a person who epitomizes my own gender, I think of the Irish poet William Butler Yeats.

Naomi: Do you think "Spoon" is a love poem?

Shuntarō Tanikawa (Japan) / The only son of a philosopher and a pianist, Shuntarō Tanikawa credits Beethoven as being the most important influence on his early writing. He was also attracted to Western cowboy movies and wrote later, "I felt great excitement when a man would go to the frontier. First, he would go all alone. He would find his own land, plant crops, build a house, get a cow, and then send for his wife and children. In this way, long before thoughts of society, a person would begin to live alone out on the last land of the West—under the blue sky." (From *The Selected Poems of Shuntarō Tanikawa*, translated by Harold Wright)

James Tate (Massachusetts) / One of James Tate's books is called *Distance from Loved Ones*. Currently a professor and collector of fine quilts, Tate grew up in Kansas City and received the Pulitzer prize for his *Selected Poems*.

Donna Trussell (Kansas) / I tend to admire outsiders, so I guess it's not surprising that when I think of "woman," I don't think of the usual female leaders. I think of Elizabeth Taylor in *Father of the Bride* and *Giant*. The characters she played were outsiders in the landscape of feminism, but to me Taylor was a priestess. The way she moved, talked, and fought for what was right taught me that gentleness and kindness were not mutually exclusive with defiance and strength.

Patty Turner (Texas) / Although as a writer I pride myself on being consistently in communication with my imagination, and although I imagine many hundreds of scenarios that may or may not turn themselves into poems, the one thing I really cannot imagine doing is writing from a male point of view. In fact, I don't think I've ever read anything, anything at all, that was written by a man in a woman's voice, or by a woman in a man's voice, that I thought I could trust. To me, gender is the one area where you must be authentic.

Leslie Ullman (Texas and New Mexican border) / My parents insisted that gender was not to be an issue in our family, but I, the daughter, experienced it as a constant struggle to be taken seriously. It was okay if I was mediocre, but not for my brother; I was not the one being groomed for action. I felt invisible, not only as a girl but in my

---

Paul: Okay, time to 'fess up. Which of the poems in this book are the ones you read and said, "I wish I had written that!"? Don't you do that when you read poems? I do it all the time. I'll tell you mine, if you tell me yours. Deal? Good. Here are mine:

1. "For My Father" by Philip Schultz
2. "My Daughter at 14: Christmas Dance, 1981" by Maria Mazziotti Gillan
3. "Once a Long Time Ago" by Phillip Lopate
4. "Dressing My Daughter" George Eklund
5. "Summer, At Home" by Mary Clark

consciousness of something no one else could or would admit.

One of Leslie Ullman's books is called *Dreams by No One's Daughter.*

Mark Vinz (Minnesota) / Every family, it seems, has certain problems in communication, which are often complicated by gender and generational differences—the subject of much of my writing.

Ellen Bryant Voigt (Vermont) / Growing up in Virginia, in the 40s and 50s, there were many gender-related protocols that mainly seemed to me silly—especially since I grew up on a farm, and farm chores are famously gender-blind, but also because my mother came from a family of strong women, five independent-minded and ambitious sisters who seemed far more interesting and substantial than the cultural ideas of white-gloved members of the Garden Club.

Anne Waldman (Colorado) / As a writer I rode on a new crest of women's consciousness at a time (late 60s) when the literary scene seemed predominantly male. I was politically active and vocal. Many women writers came into their own—on the one hand by honoring and learning from male elders (in my case, the Beat Generation and other experimenters); on the other by dancing on their corpses. This is not to sound morbid, but there was an urgency (and sense of humor) about building on the shambles and sexism of Patriarchy. I've continued writing a long epic poem for ten years that takes on male energy in all its guises. Gender definitely plays a role in my writing. There is the girl-child and the hag (as well as all that plays between) encoded in my poetry's phones and phonemes. Basically I experience that energy is both masculine and feminine in either male or female body. Our minds are empathetically inclined. As much as I write and sing out of my own body, I can also *imagine* the male. Being a scholar of gender—studying the details of the differences—can be liberating and enriching as a writer.

Ronald Wallace (Wisconsin) / The best way to get me to do something is to tell me I can't. In the 1950s, boys weren't supposed to play jacks, jump rope, sing well, or write poetry, and that was good enough for me.

Natasha Waxman (Canada and Texas) / I was lucky to have grown up in a family where my horizons were never clipped because I was female. Thus, when I came upon social expectations of female inferiority, I just thought they were ridiculous. The emperor

---

Naomi: I don't ever say "I wish I had written this" when I fall in love with a poem. Maybe it's like in that movie *Il Postino,* where the postman says a poem belongs not just to the one who wrote it but to the one who needs it. If I love a poem it's almost *more* mine than if I had written it. Is possession a "boy" thing? Personally I love *all* of the poems in this book—that's the privilege of being an editor.

always looked naked to me. Part of my work, and the work of any thinking person, is to try to screw up your eyes and look at everything in its own light, despite what you've been taught. The moment of laughing amazement is the moment of liberation. . . .

Ingrid Wendt (Oregon) / Lucky boys, they got to wear long pants every day; no one told them they couldn't turn a cartwheel because their panties would show. Even in the coldest Midwest winters, we girls wore dresses to school, and always on Sunday—and with our dresses, like the "right" accessories, a certain kind of behavior, governed by rules I never quite understood. Who wanted to be a "Little Lady?" I wanted to be "Little Lulu," my comic book heroine, finding adventures in vacant lots and snowdrifts. I wanted to live in trees (but in a dress?). I wanted to climb higher than anyone else on the rope swing my father hung in our backyard, to twirl on the parallel bars. I wanted to be like my teachers, all highly intelligent women. In their eyes I was neither tomboy nor Lady; I had an inner self separate from what I did or wore. I had ideas of my own. They mattered.

Marlys West (Louisiana and Texas) / Because I'm the oldest sibling and cousin in a big family, I associate girlhood with great power and plenty of worshipful minions. Approaching womanhood, I suffered a temporary bout of meekness.

David Wevill (Canada and Texas) / I think there are intrinsic differences between men and women, and that good poems consist of elements of both, as if there were two voices singing together, now in harmony, now in discord, but neither ever whole without the other. The difference often shows in the details.

Hugo Williams (England) / Hugo Williams begins a poem called "A Start in Life": "Of course I wanted to be an actor. I had the gold chain / like Alain Delon. I could lift one eyebrow / I didn't wear any socks. / I came home from France / with a brush cut and a sketch of myself and my father said "WHAT ARE YOU GOING TO DO?"
  Williams writes: "Except for Christina Rossetti, Elizabeth Barrett Browning, Emily Dickinson, Sylvia Plath, Elizabeth Bishop, and Marianne Moore, I didn't know women wrote poetry. Now it seems I was wrong. This is hard on a man."

Paul: By the way, kiddo, I don't see "Spoon" as a love poem. It strikes me as the opposite; it's an aloneness poem. It's a poem about being an outsider and watching as others get to do something and be something that the outsider would like to be or do. It reminds me of "All Their Names Were Vincent" with its sense of missed opportunities.

Marilyn Williams (Missouri) / There's a children's circle-song with lyrics that say, "Put your whole self in." The woman I esteem most does just that each day of her life, leaving all stereotypes of gender, class, and race behind—no room for those in her very human circle!

While physical differences are intrinsic in men and women, personal growth is a possibility for everyone. *Macho, alluring*—these are just two of the stereotypes today that need to be outgrown to find our own individuality, a deeper understanding, and hopefully, each other.

Marion Winik (New Jersey and Texas) / I have spent most of my life obsessed with love, usually in the form of some guy or another who is driving me crazy. The most productive thing I've done with this preoccupation—which I definitely blame on my gender—is to write about the various adventures and ordeals I've been through as a result. Through writing, I get the distance I need to find the meaning of my experiences, as well as the humor in them.

Nellie Wong (California) / Having grown up in a predominantly female family and having worked as a secretary for most of my life, I am conscious of being a woman in my writing. I don't set out to say I will write this because I am a woman. I write from all of me, Chinese American, a woman, a worker, and a radical.

Daisy Zamora (Nicaragua) / Poet, painter, and psychologist, Daisy Zamora was a combatant of the national Sandinista Liberation Front and served as Vice Minister of Culture after the 1979 revolution. Her book *Clean Slate* is available in the United States. She is currently active with groups devoted to women's issues in Nicaragua.

Martha Zweig (Vermont) / I learned a lot about the privileges, ordeals, and rewards of gender in our society when our daughter's father took off and I had to be "both" parents alone. Between the feminine stanzas 1 and 4, stanzas 2 and 3 explore night in terms of scientific fact—usually considered a masculine approach.

At the time this book went to press poets Mary Clark, Peter Desy, William Freedman, and Joan Fem Shaw were unavailable for comment.

Naomi: I don't particularly like being called "kiddo."

Acknowledgments

The scope of this volume made it occasionally difficult—despite sincere and sustained effort—to locate poets and/or their executors. The compilers and editor regret any omissions or errors. If you wish to contact the publisher, corrections will be made in subsequent printings. Permission to reprint copyrighted material is gratefully acknowledged to the following:

Francisco X. Alarcón, for "Ode to Tomatoes," copyright © 1995 by Francisco X. Alarcón, from *Snake Poems: An Aztec Invocation*, published by Chronicle Books, 1995. Reprinted by permission of the author.

Pamela Alexander, for "Fish Fact," copyright © 1991 by Pamela Alexander. Printed by permission of the author.

Agha Shahid Ali, for "Snowmen" and "The Previous Occupant," copyright © 1987 by Agha Shahid Ali, from *The Half-Inch Himalayas*, published by Wesleyan University Press, 1987. Reprinted by permission of the University Press of New England.

Alise Alousi, for "Medusa Cement," copyright © by Alise Alousi, first appeared in *Alternative Press*. Reprinted by permission of the author.

Christianne Balk, for "The Yellow Hills in Back," copyright © 1986 by Christianne Balk, from *Bindweed*, published by Macmillan, 1986. Reprinted by permission of the author.

Wendy Barker, for "Canning Season," copyright © 1990 by Wendy Barker, from *Winter Chickens*, by Wendy Barker, published by Corona Publishing Company. Reprinted by permission of the author.

Judith Barrington, for "Dirty Panes," copyright © 1989 by Judith Barrington, from *History and Geography*, by Judith Barrington, published by The Eighth Mountain Press. Reprinted by permission of the author and publisher.

Linda Besant, for "Telepathy," copyright © 1993 by Linda Besant. Printed by permission of the author.

Chana Bloch, for "Primer," copyright © by Chana Bloch, from *The Past Keeps Changing*, published by Sheep Meadow Press, New York, 1992. Reprinted by permission of the author.

Robert Bly, for "Taking the Hands," copyright © 1962 by Robert Bly, from *Silence in the Snowy Fields*, published by Wesleyan University Press, 1962. Reprinted by permission of the author. For "For Night Comes" by Gunnar Ekelöf, translated by Robert Bly, English translation copyright © 1975 by Robert Bly, from *Friends You Drank Some Darkness: Three Swedish Poets*, published by Beacon Press, 1975. Reprinted by permission of the translator. For "Driving My Parents Home At Christmas," copyright © 1979, 1992 by Robert

Cathy Czapla, for "Carpenter's Daughter," copyright © by Cathy Czapla, first appeared in *Samisdat*. Reprinted by permission of the author.

Andra R. Davis, for "From Him," copyright © by Andra R. Davis. Printed by permission of the author.

William Virgil Davis, for "January," copyright © 1980 by William Virgil Davis, from *One Way To Reconstruct the Scene*, published by Yale University Press. Reprinted by permission of the author and publisher.

Diana Der-Hovanessian, for "In the Orchard" and "Your Hands," by Gevorg Emin, translated by Diana Der-Hovanessian, English translations copyright © by Diana Der-Hovanessian, from *For You On New Year's Day: Selected Poems of Gevorg Emin*, published by Ohio University Press. Reprinted by permission of the translator.

Toi Derricotte, for "The Struggle" and "The Friendship," copyright © by Toi Derricote, from *Captivity*, published by University of Pittsburgh Press. Reprinted by permission of the author.

Peter Desy, for "Father Falling," copyright © by Peter Desy.

Jeannette Doob, for "My Mother's Blue Vase," copyright © by Jeannette Doob. Printed by permission of the author.

Moshe Dor, for "Before Sleep," translated by Barbara Goldberg, copyright © by Moshe Dor, published by Three Continents Press, Inc. Reprinted by permission of the publisher.

Rita Dove, for "Anti-Father," copyright © 1983 by Rita Dove, from *Museum* by Rita Dove, published by Carnegie-Mellon University Press. Reprinted by permission of the author.

Denise Duhamel, for "Feminism," copyright © by Denise Duhamel, from *Girl Soldier*, published by Garden Street Press, 1996. Reprinted by permission of the author.

Paul Durcan, for "The Lion Tamer," copyright © by Paul Durcan.

Cornelius Eady, for "I Just Wanna Testify" and "January," copyright © by Cornelius Eady. Printed by permission of the author.

George Eklund, for "Boyhood Winter," copyright © by George Eklund; for "Dressing My Daughter," copyright © by George Eklund, first appeared in *The Bellingham Review*. Reprinted by permission of the author.

Sharif S. Elmusa, for "A Little Piece of Sky," copyright © by Sharif S. Elmusa, from *Anthology of Modern Palestinian Literature*, edited by Salma Khadra Jayyusi, published by Columbia University Press, 1992. Reprinted by permission of the author.

Robert Farnsworth, for "Coloring Book," copyright © by Robert Farnsworth, from *Three or Four Hills and a Cloud*, published by Wesleyan Press, 1982. Reprinted by permission of the author.

Edward Field, for "Plant Poem," copyright © by Edward Field. Printed by permission of the author.

Karen Fiser, for "Wheelchairs That Kneel Down Like Elephants" and "Teaching Myself to Read," copyright © 1992 by Karen Fiser, from *Words Like Fate and Pain*, published by Zoland Books, Inc. Reprinted by permission of the author and publisher.

William Freedman, for "The Family," copyright © by William Freedman.

Robin Boody Galguera, for "Second Childhood" and "Alloy," copyright © by Robin Boody Galguera. Printed by permission of the author.

David Huddle, for "Two Facts," copyright © by David Huddle, from *Stopping By Home* by David Huddle, 1988. Reprinted by permission of the author.

Albert Huffstickler, for "Lament for an Old Woman," copyright © by Albert Huffstickler, first appeared in *Cedar Rock*, New Brannfels, Texas. Reprinted by permission of the author.

Gary Hyland, for "Fet Walks Melody Home," copyright © by Gary L. Hyland, from *Just Off Main*, published by Thistledown Press, Saskatuon, Canada, 1982. Reprinted by permission of the author.

David Ignatow, for "Lunchtime" copyright © 1970 by David Ignatow, from *Poems 1934-1969*, published by the Wesleyan University Press; for "The Sky Is Blue," copyright © 1964 by David Ignatow, from *Figures of the Human*, published by Wesleyan University Press. Reprinted by permission of the University Press of New England.

Yaedi E. Ignatow, for "Androgeny" and "We Were Lovers," copyright © 1996 by Yaedi E. Ignatow. Printed by permission of the author.

Paul B. Janeczko, for "How to Hug Your Three-Year-Old Daughter," copyright © 1995 by Paul B. Janeczko. Printed by permission of the author.

Cill Janeway, for "Rose," copyright © by Cill Janeway. Printed by permission of the author.

Phyllis Janowitz, for "Reach," copyright © by Phyllis Janowitz. Printed by permission of the author.

Paulette Jiles, for "Paper Matches" and "Tallness," copyright © by Paulette Jiles. Printed by permission of the author.

Roger Jones, for "*Revelations*, First Time," copyright © 1993 by Roger Jones, from *Strata*, published by Texas Review Press, Huntsville, Texas. Reprinted by permission of the author.

Diane Hina Kahanu, for "When I Was Young On an Island," copyright © by Diane Hina Kahanu. Printed by permission of the author.

Stina Katchadourian, for "On Foot I Had To Walk Through the Solar System," by Edith Södergran, translated by Stina Katchadourian, English translation copyright © by Stina Katchadourian, published by Fjord Press. Reprinted by permission of the translator.

Jane Kenyon, for "Coats," copyright © 1993 by Jane Kenyon, from *Constance*, published by Graywolf Press, Saint Paul, Minnesota. Reprinted by permission of the publisher.

Kathryn Kerr, for "Touch," copyright © by Kathryn Kerr, published by Red Herring Press and Stormline Press. Reprinted by permission of the author.

Miriam Kessler, for "All Their Names Were Vincent," copyright © by Miriam Kessler. Printed by permission of the author.

Faye Kicknosway, for "West Grand Boulevard," copyright © by Faye Kicknosway, from *Asparagus, Asparagus, Ah Sweet Asparagus*, published by Toothpaste Press, 1981. Reprinted by permission of the author.

Galway Kinnell, for "Two Set Out On Their Journey," copyright © 1980 by Galway Kinnell, from *Mortal Acts, Mortal Words*, published by Houghton Mifflin Co. Reprinted by permission of the publisher. All rights reserved.

Ron Koertge, for "The Ubiquity of the Need for Love," copyright © by Ron Koertge, first appeared in *Esquire*. Reprinted by permission of the author.

W. S. Merwin, for "The Unwritten" and "Travelling Together," copyright © 1996 by W. S. Merwin. Printed by permission of the author.

Linda Meyers, for "The Apple-Eater," copyright © by Linda Meyers, first appeared in *The Seattle Review*. Reprinted by permission of the author.

E. Ethelbert Miller, for "Dressed Up," copyright © by E. Ethelbert Miller, from *First Light: New and Selected Poems* by E. Ethelbert Miller, published by Black Classic Press, 1994. Reprinted by permission of the author.

E. K. Miller, for "My Father's Garden," by Kathy Casto, copyright © 1994 by Estella K. Casto. Printed by permission of E. K. Miller.

Jim Wayne Miller, for "A Plague of Telephones," from *The Mountains Have Come Closer* by Jim Wayne Miller, published by Appalachian Consortium Press, Boone, North Carolina 28608, 1980, 1991. Reprinted by permission of the author.

Karen Mitchell, for "Black Patent Leather Shoes," copyright © by Eighth Mountain Press. Reprinted by permission of the publisher.

Nora Mitchell, for "The Locker Room," copyright © by Nora Mitchell, from *Your Skin Is a Country*, published by Alice James Books, 1988. Reprinted by permission of the author.

Thylias Moss, for "Dennis's Sky Leopard," copyright © 1991 by Thylias Moss, from *Rainbow Remnants in Rock Bottom Ghetto Sky*, published by Persea Books. Reprinted by permission of the publisher.

Harryette Mullen, for "Momma Sayings" and "Jump City," copyright © by Harryette Mullen. Printed by permission of the author.

Eric Nelson, for "Kitchens," copyright © by Eric Nelson. Printed by permission of the author.

Marilyn Nelson, for "Bali Hai Calls Mama," copyright © 1985 by Marilyn Nelson Waniek, from *Mama's Promises* by Marilyn Nelson Waniek, published by Louisiana State University. Reprinted by permission of the author. For "April Rape," copyright © 1978 by Marilyn Nelson Waniek, from *For the Body* by Marilyn Nelson Waniek, published by Louisiana State University Press. Reprinted by permission of the publisher.

Naomi Shihab Nye, for "Elevator," copyright © by Naomi Shihab Nye. Printed by permission of the author.

Diana O'Hehir, for "Questions and Answers," copyright © by Diana O'Hehir. Printed by permission of the author.

Tommy Olofsson, for "Autobiography," copyright © 1991 by White Pine Press, translated by Jean Pearson, English translation copyright © 1991 by Jean Pearson, from *Elemental Poems*, published by White Pine Press, Freedonia, New York 14063. Reprinted by permission of the publisher.

Peter Oresick, for "The Passion and Woe in Marriage," copyright © 1990 by Peter Oresick, from *Definitions* by Peter Oresick, published by West End Press. Reprinted by permission of the author and publisher.

Gregory Orfalea, for "War," copyright © 1995 by Gregory Orfalea. Printed by permission of the author.

Gregory Orr, for "Who'd Want To Be a Man?," copyright © 1995 by Gregory Orr. Printed by permission of the author.

Grace Paley, for "Quarrel" and "Love," copyright © by Grace Paley. Printed by permission of the author.

Marylee A. Skwirz, for "Long Distance Calls," copyright © by Marylee A. Skwirz. Printed by permission of the author.

Kim R. Stafford, for "Proposal," copyright © 1976 by Kim R. Stafford, from *A Gypsy's History of the World*, published by Copper Canyon Press. Reprinted by permission of the author.

The Estate of William Stafford, for "Vocation," copyright © 1978 by William Stafford, from *Stories That Could Be True*, published by Harper & Row; for "Remembering Brother Bob," copyright © 1982 by William Stafford, from *A Glass Face In the Rain*, published by Harper & Row. Reprinted by permission of The Estate of William Stafford.

Judith W. Steinbergh, for "Letting the Parakeet Fly," copyright © 1988 by Judith W. Steinbergh, from *A Living Anytime: Prose Poems* by Judith W. Steinbergh, published by Talking Stone Press, Brookline, Massachusetts. Reprinted by permission of the author.

Gerald Stern, for "Romance," copyright © by Gerald Stern, from *Paradise Poems*, published by Harper; for "Cow Worship," copyright © by Gerald Stern, from *Red Coat*. Reprinted by permission of the author.

Ruth Stone, for "Pokeberries," copyright © by Ruth Stone. Printed by permission of the author.

Anna Swir, for "The Youngest Children of an Angel" and "Astonishment," translated by Czeslaw Milosz with Leonard Nathan, English translations copyright © 1996 by Czeslaw Milosz with Leonard Nathan, from *Speaking To My Body* by Anna Swir, published by Copper Canyon Press, Port Townsend, Washington 98368. Reprinted by permission of the publisher.

Arthur Sze, for "The Shapes of Leaves," copyright © 1995 by Arthur Sze, from *Archipelago* by Arthur Sze, published by Copper Canyon Press, 1995. Reprinted by permission of the author.

James Tate, for "A Missed Opportunity," copyright © 1994 by James Tate, from *Worshipful Community of Fletchers* by James Tate, first published by The Ecco Press in 1994. Reprinted by permission of the publisher.

Donna Trussell, for "This Woman," copyright © by Donna Trussell, first appeared in *The Quarterly* #17, Spring 1991; for "Snow," copyright © by Donna Trussell, first appeared in *Poetry Northwest* , Autumn 1987. Reprinted by permission of the author.

Patty Turner, for "Looking For Him," copyright © by Patty Turner. Printed by permission of the author.

Leslie Ullman, for "Peace," copyright © 1987, from *Dreams By No One's Daughter*, published by the University of Pittsburgh Press. Reprinted by permission of the publisher.

Mark Vinz, for "Sins of the Fathers," copyright © by Mark Vinz; for "Passages," copyright © 1989 by Mark Vinz, from *Mixed Blessings*, published by Spoon River Poetry Press. Reprinted by permission of the author.

Ellen Bryant Voigt, for "The Field Trip,"copyright © 1987 by Ellen Bryant Voigt, from *The Lotus Flowers* by Ellen Bryant Voigt, published by W. W. Norton & Company, Inc. Reprinted by permission of the author and publisher.

Anne Waldman, for "Two Men," copyright © by Anne Waldman, from *Kill Or Cure*, published by Penguin Poets, 1994. Reprinted by permission of the author.

Ronald Wallace, for "Wild Strawberries," copyright © by Ronald Wallace, first appeared in *Quarterly West: A Magazine of Literature*; for "The Real Thing," copyright © 1981 by Ronald Wallace, from *Plums, Stones, Kisses and Hooks* by Ronald Wallace, published by the University of Missouri Press. Reprinted by permission of the author and publishers.

Natasha Waxman, for "War Rug," copyright © 1995 by Natasha Waxman. Printed by permission of the author.

Ingrid Wendt, for "The Teacher I Wanted To Be," copyright © 1987 by Ingrid Wendt, from *Singing the Mozart Requiem*, published by Breitenbush Books, 1987. Reprinted by permission of the author.

Marlys West, for "The Exciting New Concept of Art Therapy," copyright © by Marlys West, from *Evangeline Was a Beauty Queen and Other Stories*. Reprinted by permission of the author.

David Wevill, for "Namelessness" and "The Mystery," copyright © by David Wevill. Printed by permission of the author.

Hugo Williams, for "Gone Away," copyright © by Hugo Williams. Printed by permission of the author.

Marilyn M. Williams, for "Images," copyright © by Marilyn Williams. Printed by permission of the author.

Marion Winik, for "Foreign Exchange," copyright © 1981 by Marion Winik. Printed by permission of the author.

Nellie Wong, for "Where Are You Going?" copyright © by Nellie Wong, from *The Death of Long Steam Lady*, published by West End Press, 1986. Reprinted by permission of the author.

Harold Wright, for "August" and "Everyone," by Shuntaro Tanikawa, translated by Harold Wright, English translations copyright © by Harold Wright, published by North Point Press. Reprinted by permission of the translator.

Daisy Zamora, for "To Be a Woman," copyright © 1993 by Daisy Zamora, English translation copyright © by Margaret Randall and Elinor Randall, from *Clean Slate: New and Selected Poems*, published by Curbstone Press. Reprinted by permission of the publisher.

Martha Zweig, for "Dark Song," copyright © by Martha Zweig, from *Powers*, published by the Vermont Council on the Arts, 1976. Reprinted by permission of the author.

The Robert Bly excerpt on page 21 is from *Meditations to the Insatiable Soul*, Harper Perennial, 1994.

Index of poems

Index to Female Poets

Index to Male Poets